Collins

KS3
Science
Year 8
Workbook

Ian Honeysett, Sam Holyman and
Lynn Pharaoh

About this Workbook

There are three Collins workbooks for KS3 Science:
Year 7 Science ISBN 9780008553722
Year 8 Science ISBN 9780008553739
Year 9 Science ISBN 9780008553746

Together they provide topic-based practice for all the skills and content on the Programme of Study for Key Stage 3 Science.

Questions for each topic have been organised into sections that test different **skills**.

- Vocabulary Builder
- Maths Skills
- Testing Understanding
- Working Scientifically
- Science in Use

Found throughout the book, the **QR codes** can be scanned on your smartphone. Each QR code links to a video working through the solution to one of the questions or question parts on the double-page spread.

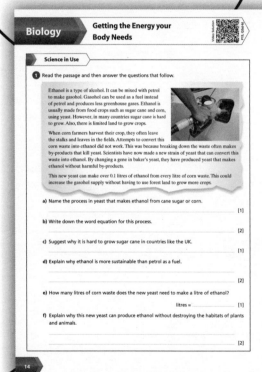

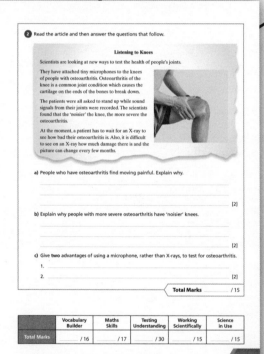

Track your progress by recording your marks in the box at the end of each skills section and the summary box at the end of each topic.

The **answers** are included at the back of the book so that you can mark your own work.

If you get a question wrong, make sure you read the answer carefully so that you understand where you went wrong.

Helpful tips are also included.

Contents

Biology

Chemistry

Physics

Answers

Acknowledgements

The authors and publisher are grateful to the copyright holders for permission to use quoted materials and images.

All Images are ©Shutterstock.com or ©HarperCollinsPublishers

Every effort has been made to trace copyright holders and obtain their permission for the use of copyright material. The authors and publisher will gladly receive information enabling them to rectify any error or omission in subsequent editions. All facts are correct at time of going to press.

Published by Collins
An imprint of HarperCollinsPublishers
1 London Bridge Street
London SE1 9GF

HarperCollinsPublishers
Macken House
39/40 Mayor Street Upper
Dublin 1
D01 C9W8
Ireland

© HarperCollinsPublishers Limited 2023

ISBN 9780008553739

10 9 8 7 6 5 4 3

All rights reserved. No part of this publication may be reproduced, stored in a retrieval system, or transmitted, in any form or by any means, electronic, mechanical, photocopying, recording or otherwise, without the prior permission of Collins.

British Library Cataloguing in Publication Data.

A CIP record of this book is available from the British Library.

Publisher: Clare Souza
Commissioning: Richard Toms
Authors: Ian Honeysett (Biology), Sam Holyman (Chemistry) and Lynn Pharaoh (Physics)
Project Editors: Charlotte Christensen and Katie Galloway
Cover Design: Kevin Robbins and Sarah Duxbury
Inside Concept Design: Sarah Duxbury and Paul Oates
Text Design and Layout: Contentra Technologies
Production: Emma Wood
Printed in India by Multivista Global Pvt. Ltd.

This book contains FSC™ certified paper and other controlled sources to ensure responsible forest management.

For more information visit:
www.harpercollins.co.uk/green

Vocabulary Builder

1 Draw lines to join each part of the body with its correct function.

Part of the body	Function

Cartilage	Joins muscles to bones
Ligaments	Contracts to cause bones to move
Tendons	Stops bone rubbing on bone
Muscles	Holds bones together at joints

[3]

2 This question is about joints, muscles and respiration.

For each part, put a tick to show if each statement is **true** or **false**.

	True	False	
a) Knee joint			
is a ball and socket joint	☐	☐	
is bent or straightened by antagonistic muscles	☐	☐	[2]
b) Bicep and tricep muscles			
are antagonistic muscles	☐	☐	
cause movement at the elbow	☐	☐	[2]
c) Glycogen			
is found in muscles	☐	☐	
is a store of glucose	☐	☐	[2]
d) Mitochondria			
are only found in animal cells	☐	☐	
contain enzymes for respiration	☐	☐	[2]

3 For each term, circle the word or words that completes the definition.

a) Aerobic respiration:

The process that releases energy from food using **carbon dioxide / oxygen / lactic acid**. [1]

b) Fermentation:

A type of anaerobic respiration in yeast that produces **ethanol / water / lactic acid.**   [1]

c) Osteoporosis:

A condition that results in bones being more likely to **rub together / fracture / bend.**   [1]

d) Bone marrow:

A soft substance in bones that produces **mitochondria / blood cells / glycogen.**   [1]

e) Oxygen debt:

The extra oxygen that is needed after exercise to break down **lactic acid / ethanol / glycogen.**   [1]

Total Marks .... / 16

Maths Skills

1 Doctors can measure the density of a patient's leg bones. They can give a person a **z** score depending on the density of the patient's bones.

Graph 1 shows the percentage chance of patients with different **z** scores having a hip fracture in the next ten years.

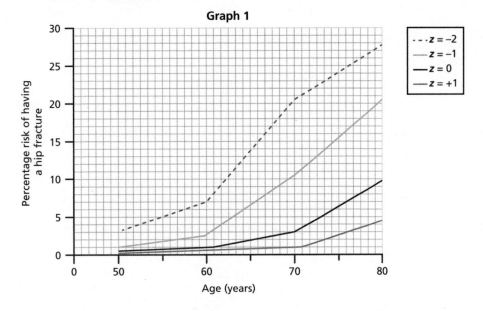

Graph 1

a) Complete these sentences using the information from the graph.

As a patient gets older, their risk of having a hip fracture ....

A patient who has a more negative **z** score is .... likely to have a hip fracture than a patient with a positive **z** score.

A 70-year-old patient with a **z** score of −2 is .... times more likely to have a fracture than if their **z** score was −1.   [3]

b) Graph 1 is for female patients.

Suggest why a different graph is needed for male patients.

.... [1]

c) Doctors also have a graph that helps them to decide what advice to give to their patients.

They can advise that an operation might be needed or advise a patient to reduce their risk of a fracture.

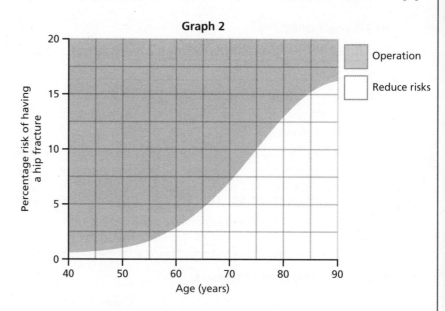

Graph 2

Operation
Reduce risks

y-axis: Percentage risk of having a hip fracture

x-axis: Age (years)

i) What advice might a doctor give to a 50-year-old patient who has a 5% risk of a fracture?

.... [1]

ii) What advice might a doctor give to an 80-year-old patient who has a 5% risk of a fracture?

.... [1]

iii) Suggest **one** reason why the advice shown in the graph is different for these two patients in parts **i)** and **ii)**, even though they have the same percentage risk.

....

.... [1]

iv) A 70-year-old woman has a **z** score of −1. Use both Graph 1 and Graph 2 to work out what advice a doctor should give to the woman about her hip.

Explain how you worked out your answer.

....

.... [2]

2 A winemaker is making some wine by fermenting grape juice.

During the fermentation, the winemaker measures:
- the concentration of sugar in the wine
- the concentration of ethanol in the wine.

The table shows the concentration of sugar in the wine during fermentation.

Time (days)	Concentration of sugar in the wine (g per 200 ml)
0	40
2	40
4	37
8	20
12	10
16	4

a) The winemaker has plotted the concentration of ethanol on a grid.

Plot the concentration of sugar during the fermentation on the same grid. Draw a smooth curve through your points for sugar concentration.

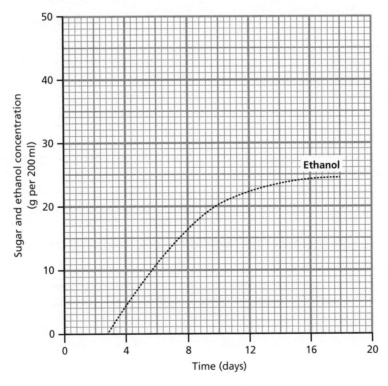

[3]

b) Describe how the concentration of ethanol changes during the fermentation.

_____

_____ [2]

c) At what time in the fermentation is the concentration of ethanol the same as the concentration of sugar?

time = _____ days   [1]

d) The winemaker is fermenting 5000 ml of grape juice in a glass jar.

Calculate how much sugar will be left in the jar after 16 days of fermentation.

quantity = _____ g   [2]

Total Marks _____ / 17

Testing Understanding

1 Draw lines to join each bone of the body with its correct feature.

Bone	Feature
Cranium	Has a disc of cartilage between each bone
Femur	Protects the brain from damage
Pelvis	Contains sockets for ball and socket joints
Vertebra	Has a round end for a ball and socket joint

[3]

2 The table shows the winning times for some different running events at the Mexico City Olympics and the London Olympics.

| Event | Winning time (s) | |
	Mexico City, 1968	London, 2012
200 metres	20	20
5000 metres	823	822
10 000 metres	1712	1620

a) How much faster was the winning 10 000 m time in London?

time = _____ seconds [1]

b) Mexico City is over 2000 metres above sea level. That means that there is less oxygen available in the air.

Complete these sentences to show the reasons for the differences between the times.

In Mexico City, the longer the distance the athletes had to run, the _____ the winning time was compared to in London.

This is because athletes usually use anaerobic respiration when running short distance events but use aerobic respiration to run long distance events.

If long distance runners use anaerobic respiration, then _____ builds up in their muscles. This causes the muscles to _____ and makes them run slower.

In Mexico City, long distance runners found it harder to use aerobic respiration because

of the low levels of _____ in the air. [4]

c) When people live at high altitude in places like Mexico City, the number of red blood cells in their blood can increase from 5 million to 7.5 million per cm^3 of blood.

i) Calculate the percentage of red blood cells at high altitude compared to the usual number.

percentage = _____ % [2]

ii) Explain why long-distance runners often live and train at high altitude before competing in events.

_____

_____

_____

_____ [3]

3 The table gives two properties of some tissues of the human skeleton.

Tissue	Stiffness (arbitrary units)	Strength (arbitrary units)
Bone	14 000	180
Cartilage	15	1
Ligament	20	110
Tendon	200	100

a) Calculate how many times stiffer bone is, compared to tendon.

.... (times) [2]

b) Ligament and tendon are stronger than cartilage.

Explain why they need to be so strong.

....

....

[2]

c) In the sea, the water helps to support animals.
Some fish, like sharks, have a skeleton made from cartilage rather than bone.

Explain why land animals do not have skeletons made of cartilage.

....

....

[2]

4 Small amounts of wine can be made in a glass jar.

The diagram shows yeast fermenting fruit juice in order to make wine.

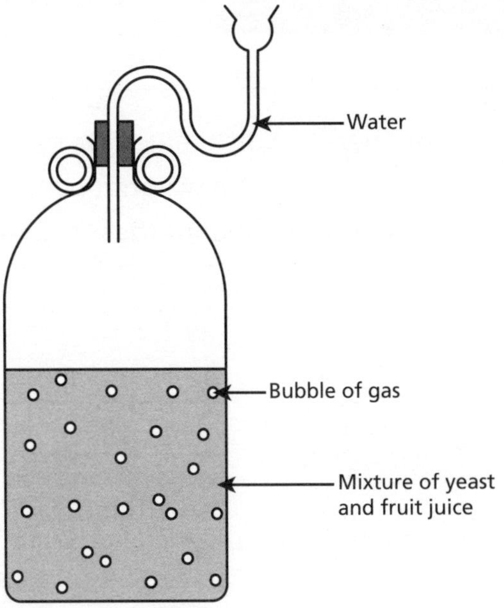

a) Which substance in the fruit juice is the yeast using for fermentation?

_____ [1]

b) What is the main gas in the bubbles?

_____ [1]

c) The water in the air lock stops microbes entering from the air.

Explain why this is important in winemaking.

_____

_____ [2]

Water

Bubble of gas

Mixture of yeast and fruit juice

5 The diagram shows some of the muscles and bones in the human arm.

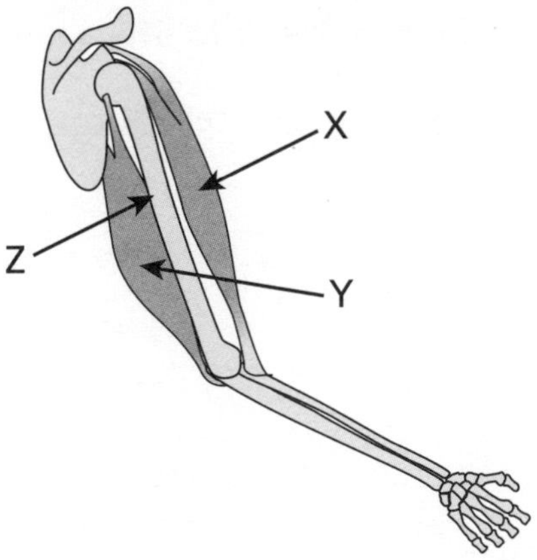

X

Z

Y

a) i) Give the names of structures **X**, **Y** and **Z** using the options from the box.

bicep	humerus	tricep	quadriceps	radius	ulna

X = _____

Y = _____

Z = _____ [3]

ii) Which structure **X**, **Y** or **Z**, contracts to lift the hand? _____ [1]

b) There are different ways to measure the strength of the bicep muscle in the arm. One way is to lift a weight up and down at a steady pace. You count the number of lifts that can be done until the weight is no longer lifted at a steady pace.

The strength of the bicep is then given by this formula.

strength = (0.033 × number of lifts × mass of the weight) + mass of the weight

Kaye has a bicep strength of 65. Her friend Jo lifts a weight of mass 60 kg six times.

Work out which friend has the strongest bicep. Show how you worked out your answer.

_____

_____

_____ [3]

Total Marks _____ / 30

Working Scientifically

1 Henry wants to investigate the effect of exercise on his hand.

This is his method:
1. Squeeze a ball in his hand as fast as possible for 90 seconds.
2. Count how many times the ball is squeezed in each 15-second interval.
3. Repeat four times and calculate the mean (average) for each time interval.

The following table shows the results:

Time (seconds)	Number of squeezes				
	Round 1	Round 2	Round 3	Round 4	Mean (average)
0–15	35	34	36	31	34
15–30	34	33	35	30	33
30–45	33	52	34	29	32
45–60	25	25	24	22	24
60–75	23	23	22	20	22
75–90	20	20	19	17	

a) What piece of equipment does Henry need to use apart from the ball?

_____ [1]

b) Which is the independent variable in the investigation? Tick **one** box.

The time since the start of the exercise ☐

The number of squeezes in 15 seconds ☐

The size of the dent made in the ball when squeezed ☐ [1]

c) Calculate the mean of the results for the 75–90 second interval.
Show your working and then write your answer in the table. [2]

d) When the mean was calculated for the 30–45 second interval, one of the results was not used. Which result was not used and why?

_____

_____ [2]

e) Describe how Henry would show his results as a graph.

_____

_____ [2]

f) Complete these sentences about the results.

Towards the end of the investigation, the mean number of squeezes in each interval went

_____. The largest change was between _____ seconds and _____ seconds.

At the start of the experiment, Henry's muscles were using _____ respiration to

provide energy to squeeze the ball. Towards the end of the investigation his muscles were

not receiving enough _____ gas. Therefore, _____ was building up in his

muscles making them hurt. This substance is made by _____ respiration. [7]

Total Marks _____ / 15

Science in Use

1 Read the passage and then answer the questions that follow.

Ethanol is a type of alcohol. It can be mixed with petrol to make gasohol. Gasohol can be used as a fuel instead of petrol and produces less greenhouse gases. Ethanol is usually made from food crops such as sugar cane and corn, using yeast. However, in many countries sugar cane is hard to grow. Also, there is limited land to grow crops.

When corn farmers harvest their crop, they often leave the stalks and leaves in the fields. Attempts to convert this corn waste into ethanol did not work. This was because breaking down the waste often makes by-products that kill yeast. Scientists have now made a new strain of yeast that can convert this waste into ethanol. By changing a gene in baker's yeast, they have produced yeast that makes ethanol without harmful by-products.

This new yeast can make over 0.1 litres of ethanol from every litre of corn waste. This could increase the gasohol supply without having to use forest land to grow more crops.

a) Name the process in yeast that makes ethanol from cane sugar or corn.

.... [1]

b) Write down the word equation for this process.

.... [2]

c) Suggest why it is hard to grow sugar cane in countries like the UK.

.... [1]

d) Explain why ethanol is more sustainable than petrol as a fuel.

....

.... [2]

e) How many litres of corn waste does the new yeast need to make a litre of ethanol?

litres = ... [1]

f) Explain why this new yeast can produce ethanol without destroying the habitats of plants and animals.

....

.... [2]

2 Read the article and then answer the questions that follow.

Listening to Knees

Scientists are looking at new ways to test the health of people's joints.

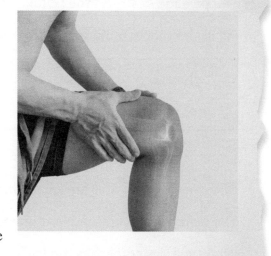

They have attached tiny microphones to the knees of people with osteoarthritis. Osteoarthritis of the knee is a common joint condition which causes the cartilage on the ends of the bones to break down.

The patients were all asked to stand up while sound signals from their joints were recorded. The scientists found that the 'noisier' the knee, the more severe the osteoarthritis.

At the moment, a patient has to wait for an X-ray to see how bad their osteoarthritis is. Also, it is difficult to see on an X-ray how much damage there is and the picture can change every few months.

a) People who have osteoarthritis find moving painful. Explain why.

....

....

.... [2]

b) Explain why people with more severe osteoarthritis have 'noisier' knees.

....

....

.... [2]

c) Give **two** advantages of using a microphone, rather than X-rays, to test for osteoarthritis.

1. ....

2. .... [2]

Total Marks .... / 15

	Vocabulary Builder	Maths Skills	Testing Understanding	Working Scientifically	Science in Use
Total Marks	.... / 16	.... / 17	.... / 30	.... / 15	.... / 15

Vocabulary Builder

1 The passage describes the uptake and movement of water through a plant.

Fill in the spaces using words from the box.

glucose	minerals	photosynthesis	palisade	respiration
root hair cells	stomata	transpiration	waxy cuticle	xylem

Water is taken up into the plant by special structures called ....

Dissolved in the water are small amounts of ....

The water passes up the plant in a tissue called ....

When the water reaches the leaves, it diffuses through structures called ....
into the air.

This process is called ....   [5]

2 Fertilisers are usually marked with NPK values.

Which elements do NPK stand for in the fertiliser?

Choose the elements from the list in the box.

krypton	neon	nickel	nitrogen	phosphorus	potassium	sodium

N = ...   P = ...   K = ...   [3]

3 Draw lines to join each ecological term to the correct definition.

Ecological term	Definition

Ecological term		Definition
Ecosystem		An area where organisms live
Habitat		All the same type of organisms living in the same area
Population		All the organisms living in the same area
Community		All the living organisms and the non-living material in an area

[3]

4 This question is about food chains. For each statement, put a tick to show if the statement is **true** or **false**.

a) **Producers:**

	True	False	
make their own food	☐	☐	
are part of the first trophic level	☐	☐	
eat primary consumers	☐	☐	[3]

b) **Secondary consumers:**

	True	False	
are photosynthetic	☐	☐	
are plants	☐	☐	
are eaten by tertiary consumers	☐	☐	[3]

c) **Primary consumers:**

	True	False	
can be green plants or animals	☐	☐	
are part of the second trophic level	☐	☐	
eat producers	☐	☐	[3]

Total Marks _____ / 20

Maths Skills

1 Tomatoes can be grown by intensive farming or by organic farming.

The graph shows the energy involved in both types of farming to grow one tonne of tomatoes.

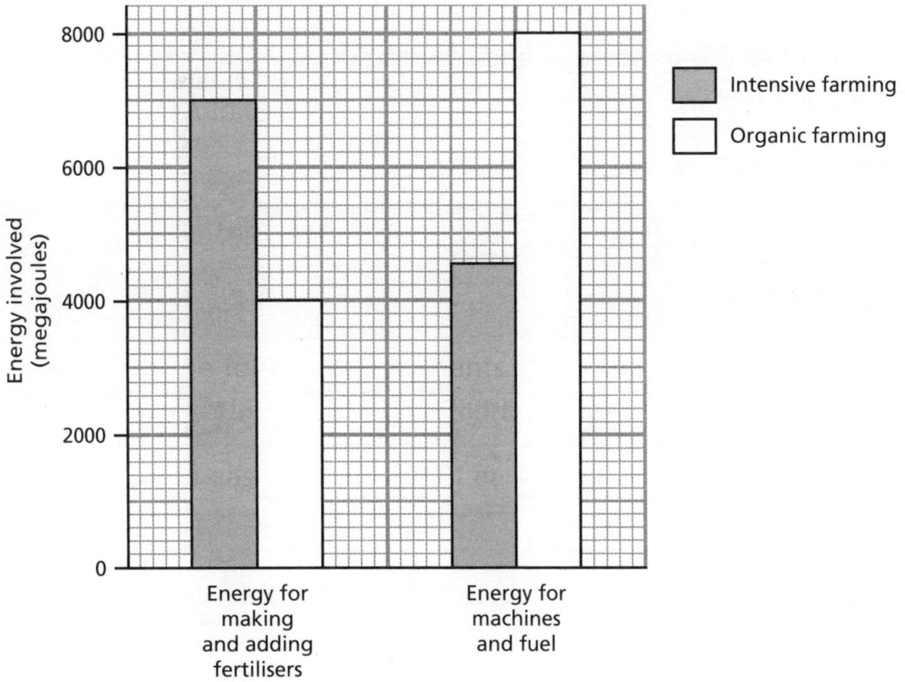

a) i) How much energy is involved in organic farming for making and adding fertilisers?

energy = _____ megajoules [1]

ii) How much more energy is involved in intensive farming than in organic farming for making and adding fertilisers?

energy = _____ megajoules [1]

b) Calculate the total amount of energy involved in organic farming to produce one tonne of tomatoes.

energy = _____ megajoules [2]

c) Which type of farming involves most energy to produce one tonne of tomatoes?

Explain your answer.

_____

_____ [2]

2 Bea sets up an experiment to see if carbon dioxide concentration affects the rate of photosynthesis in pondweed.

She changed the mass of sodium hydrogen carbonate in the water.

Sodium hydrogen carbonate provides the pondweed with carbon dioxide.

Bea pointed a light at the pondweed and counted the number of bubbles of oxygen given off in one-minute intervals.

The table shows her results.

Mass of sodium hydrogen carbonate (g)	Number of bubbles of oxygen given off			
	1st minute	2nd minute	3rd minute	Mean (average)
0.0	4	6	5	5
0.2	18	22	20	20
0.4	36	34	35	35
0.6	38	38	12	38
0.8	_____	39	38	39

a) Calculate the number of bubbles during the 1st minute for 0.8 g of sodium hydrogen carbonate. Write your result in the table. [1]

b) When Bea counted the bubbles with 0.6 g of sodium hydrogen carbonate, she thinks that the light had been moved after the 2nd minute.

Why might she think this?

.... [1]

c) Plot Bea's results for the mean number of bubbles on the grid.

Draw a best curve through the points.

Mean number of bubbles given off in one minute (y-axis, 0 to 60)
Mass of sodium hydrogen carbonate (g) (x-axis, 0 to 0.8)

[3]

d) Complete these sentences to describe the results of Bea's experiment.

As the mass of sodium hydrogen carbonate increases, the number of bubbles given

off ....

This is because there is more .... available to the plant to use in the

process of ....

At high concentrations of sodium hydrogen carbonate, the number of bubbles given

off starts to .... [4]

Testing Understanding

1 A farmer is growing wheat in a field. The diagram shows a food web from the field.

Wheat → Greenfly → Ladybird → Blue tit

Wheat → Mouse

a) Which organism in the food web is a secondary consumer? .... [1]

b) The farmer sprays his field with pesticide to kill the greenfly.

   i) Suggest why the farmer did this.

   ....

   .... [2]

   ii) Explain what effects this might have on the other organisms in the food chain.

   ....

   ....

   .... [3]

2 The diagram shows a section through a leaf from a plant that loses its leaves in winter (deciduous).

a) Give the names of the layers of cells labelled **A**, **B**, **C** and **D**. Choose the names from the box.

> lower epidermis   palisade mesophyll
>
> spongy mesophyll   upper epidermis
>
> waxy cuticle

A = ...

B = ...

C = ...

D = ... [4]

b) Which layer of cells, **A**, **B**, **C** or **D**, has the most chloroplasts? .... [1]

c) This diagram shows a section through a leaf from a plant that keeps its leaves during winter (evergreen).

Describe **two** differences between the evergreen leaf and the deciduous leaf.

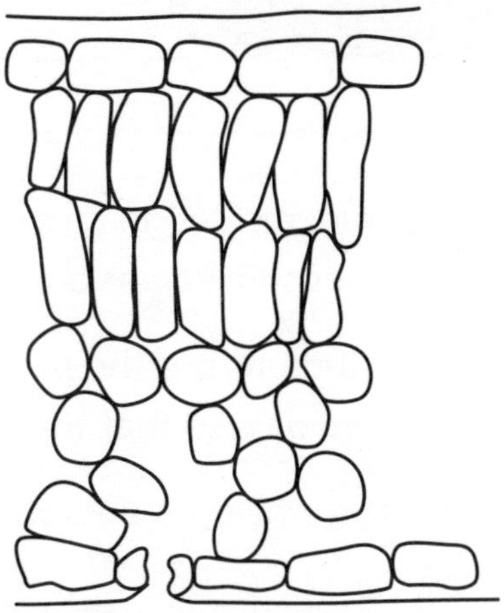

1. ....

....

2. ....

.... **[2]**

3 In China, rice plants are grown in large, flooded fields. Fish are farmed in the same fields. The fish provide the people with extra food.

Recently the Chinese have started to add a small plant called azolla to the fields. The azolla is food for the fish.

a) Draw a food web for the flooded fields. In your food web include rice plants, azolla, fish and humans.

[2]

b) The fish help the rice to grow by producing nitrogen-rich faeces.

Explain how this helps the rice plants to grow.

....

.... **[2]**

c) As well as eating azolla, the fish also eat insects that are parasites of the rice plants.

Explain why this is helpful for the farmers.

....

....

.... **[2]**

4 Some students design an experiment using a potted plant. The plant has variegated leaves. This means some areas are green and some are white.

Green area

White area

a) The students put the potted plant in a closed cupboard for two days so that the leaves do not contain any starch.

Explain why the leaves will not now contain starch.

....

....

.... [2]

b) The students now cover part of the leaf with black cardboard. The cardboard has a hole cut out. They leave the leaf in the light for 12 hours. They then remove the cardboard and test the leaf for starch.

Black cardboard over both sides of the leaf

Hole cut in black cardboard

i) What chemical would they use to test the leaf for starch?

Tick **one** box.

biuret reagent ☐

Benedict's reagent ☐

iodine solution ☐

limewater ☐ [1]

ii) Put a circle around the diagram that shows the correct results of the test.

A   B   C   D   [1]

iii) Explain the pattern of black areas seen in the results.

....

....

.... [3]

Total Marks .... / 26

1 Some students set up an experiment to measure the loss of water from plant shoots.

They used four shoots from the same plant. Each shoot had six leaves.

They removed the leaves from one of the shoots and spread grease over the surfaces of some of the other leaves.

The diagram shows how the shoots were set up in test tubes of water.

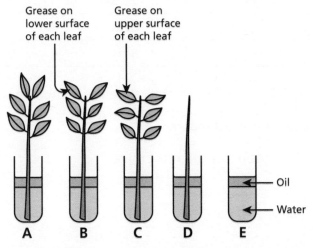

The students measured the mass of each of the tubes and contents at the start of the investigation.

Then, after two days, they measured the mass again.

They calculated the loss in mass from each tube and used this as a measure of how much water each shoot had lost.

a) i) Write down **two** ways that the students made their experiment a fair test.

1. ....

2. .... [2]

ii) Why did the students put oil on the water in each tube? Tick **one** box.

To stop microorganisms getting into the water ☐

To stop water evaporating from the test tube ☐

To stop carbon dioxide diffusing into the water ☐ [1]

iii) Why did the students include test tube **E** in their experiment?

.... [1]

b) The table shows the students' results.

Tube	Mass at start (g)	Mass at end (g)	Loss in mass (g)
A	70.1	67.9	2.2
B	72.1	71.4	0.7
C	72.4	70.8	
D	62.0	61.8	
E	61.1	61.1	0.0

i) Calculate the two missing values in the table. Write them in the table. [2]

ii) Which test tube lost the most mass? .... [1]

iii) Explain why this test tube lost the most mass.

....

....

....

[2]

iv) Explain why test tube **C** lost more mass than test tube **B**.

....

....

....

[2]

2 Duckweed is a small plant that floats on the surface of ponds. Each plant has one leaf and it usually reproduces by dividing into two.

Carlos investigates the effect of garden fertiliser on the reproduction rate of duckweed.

This is his method:
1. Put pondwater in four different beakers.
2. Dissolve 1 g of fertiliser in the pondwater.
3. Add five duckweed plants to each beaker.
4. Repeat this with beakers using 2 g and 3 g of fertiliser.
5. Leave the beakers for 10 days.
6. Count how many plants are in each jar.

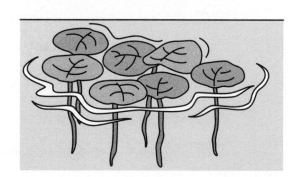

The following is Carlos's results table.

Mass of garden fertiliser added (g)	Number of duckweed plants after 10 days				
	Beaker 1	Beaker 2	Beaker 3	Beaker 4	Mean
1	6	5	7	6	6
2	12	14	11	11	12
3	13	16	11	12	....

a) Calculate the mean number of duckweed plants in the beakers with 3 g of fertiliser.
Show your working and write your answer in the table. [2]

b) Describe how increasing the fertiliser affected the rate of reproduction.

....

....

.... [2]

c) All the beakers were given the same amount of light for 10 days.
Explain why this is important.

....

.... [2]

Total Marks .... / 17

Science in Use

1 Read the passage about the conservation of the white-clawed crayfish and answer the questions.

The white-clawed crayfish has become one of the UK's most endangered species. This has happened because of the introduction into the UK of the North American crayfish. This species produces lots of offspring and eats almost anything, from dead material water plants to small invertebrates.

The white-clawed crayfish numbers have decreased to about 10% of their original numbers in all areas.

A number of the white-clawed crayfish have been bred at Bristol Zoo Gardens. Now they are being released into a small pond that has been made near Bristol. The location of the pond is being kept secret.

One scientist said, 'We are hoping that most of the crayfish will survive in this man-made pond because they are free of the dangers that they would face in a natural pond or river'.

a) Explain what the term **endangered** means.

....

.... **[2]**

b) Suggest **two** ways that the North American crayfish may be causing the numbers of white-clawed crayfish to drop.

1. ....

2. .... **[2]**

c) In one area, there were 5000 white-clawed crayfish before the North American crayfish arrived.

Calculate the number of white-clawed crayfish that are present now. Show your working.

number = ... **[2]**

d) Suggest why the location of the pond where the crayfish are being released is being kept secret.

....

.... **[2]**

e) Scientists think that the crayfish are more likely to survive in a pond that has been built for them, rather than in a natural pond or river.

Suggest why this might be true.

....

....

.... **[2]**

Total Marks .... **/ 10**

	Vocabulary Builder	Maths Skills	Testing Understanding	Working Scientifically	Science in Use
Total Marks	.... / 20	.... / 15	.... / 26	.... / 17	.... / 10

1 Match each key word to the description of the mixture that they form.

Key word	Definition

| Emulsion | Gas bubbles trapped in a liquid |

| Colloid | Liquid particles in a solid |

| Foam | Two liquids (one water based and one oil based) |

| Gel | Liquid or solid particles in a gas |

| Aerosol | Different states of matter that are dispersed together |

[4]

2 Complete the sentences about how scientific theories are developed using the terms from the box. You can use the terms once, more than once or not at all.

| scientific theory | peer review | repeat | evidence |
| scientific law | hypothesis | prediction | |

A _____ aims to explain observations about the world around us. By using scientific knowledge and experiments, evidence is collected to support the ideas. _____ then happens, where other scientists examine the evidence, _____ the experiments and discuss any evidence they have found to refine the _____. When many scientists agree and many repeated experiments give the same outcomes, the hypothesis becomes known as a _____.

[5]

3 The diagram below shows the different physical changes that describe when substances change state.

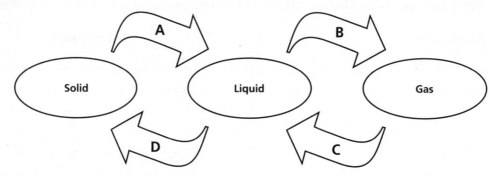

a) Give the letter that describes:

   i) melting .... [1]

   ii) boiling .... [1]

   iii) freezing .... [1]

   iv) evaporation .... [1]

   v) condensing .... [1]

b) Add a labelled arrow on to the diagram to show sublimation. [1]

4 What does **concentration** mean? Circle the letter for the correct definition.

A: The measure of the number of solute particles in a given volume of solvent.

B: The measure of the average force of collisions from a liquid or gas over the area of the container's sides.

C: The measure of the number of solvent particles in a given volume of solution.

D: The measure of the mass in a certain volume of a substance. [1]

5 Which of the following statements about **latent heat** are **true** (T) and which are **false** (F)?

Write **T** or **F** in the spaces provided.

a) Latent heat is the 'extra heat' needed to cause a substance to melt. .... [1]

b) Latent heat makes intermolecular forces between
   the particles in a substance. .... [1]

c) The stronger the intermolecular forces between the particles,
   the more latent heat is needed to melt the substance. .... [1]

Total Marks .... / 19

1) Density is a measure of how many particles there are in a given space.

a) What is the formula that connects density, mass and volume?

_____ [1]

b) What is the density of 14 g of bricks that has a volume of 10 cm^3?
Show your working and give the units in your answer.

density = _____ [3]

c) Water has a density of 1 g/cm^3.

What is the mass of 10 cm^3 of water? Show your working and give the units in your answer.

mass = _____ [4]

d) What is the volume of 55 g of pure water?
Show your working and give the units in your answer.

volume = _____ [4]

e) Cooking oil has a density of 0.911 g/cm^3.

When cooking oil is added to water, will it float or sink? Explain your answer.

_____

_____ [2]

2 A student was investigating a solid and the effect of changing temperature. They put the solid into a boiling tube and gently heated it for 8 minutes, recording the temperature using a data logger. The graph from the data logger is shown below.

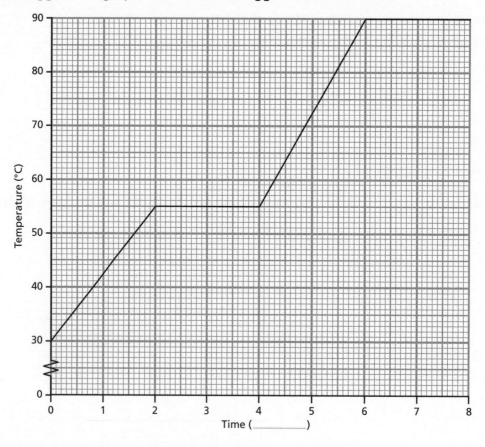

a) Complete the *x*-axis label by adding the unit. [1]

b) What was the melting point of the substance that the student was investigating? .... [1]

c) What was the boiling point of the substance that the student was investigating? .... [1]

d) What state was the substance in after 1 minute of being heated? .... [1]

e) What state was the substance in at 70°C? .... [1]

3 The Mohs Hardness Scale can be used to measure the hardness of materials on a scale of 1 to 10. The table below shows the hardness of different types of glass.

Material	Hardness
Sodalime	6
Glass window	5.5
Borosilicate	7.5

a) Order the materials from hardest to softest.

_____ [1]

b) Round the glass window hardness to the nearest whole number. _____ [1]

c) Give the borosilicate hardness to one significant figure. _____ [1]

d) Calculate the average (mean) hardness of all three types of glass using the information from the table. Give your answer to 2 decimal places.

hardness = _____ [3]

4 Gases can dissolve in water. The graph below shows how solubility of oxygen changes as temperature changes.

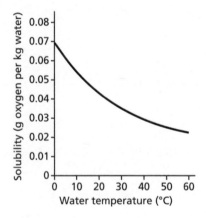

a) What is the dependent variable? _____ [1]

b) What is the unit of the independent variable? _____ [1]

c) What is the trend shown in the data?

_____ [1]

5 Jasvinder wanted to investigate the state of different substances at room temperature (25°C). He looked up the melting and boiling points.

Complete Jasvinder's table to show the state of each substance at room temperature.

Substance	Melting point (°C)	Boiling point (°C)	State at room temperature
Mercury	−38.8	356.7	**a)** _____
Sulfur	112.8	444.6	**b)** _____
Sulfur dioxide	−72.0	−10.0	**c)** _____

[3]

Total Marks _____ / 31

Testing Understanding

1 Betty took a small sample of carbon powder and added it to a drop of oil to make a wet mount on a microscope slide. A sketch of what Betty saw under the microscope is below.

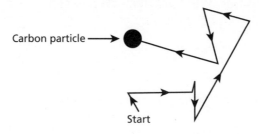

Carbon particle ⟶

Start

a) Describe Betty's observations.

.... [2]

b) What is the name of the process that describes how the carbon particle moves?

.... [1]

c) Use Betty's sketch to help you explain what causes pressure in a liquid.

....

....

.... [3]

2 Xing opened a perfume bottle in the middle of the room. He noticed that the smell spread out around the room and made the room smell nice.

a) What is the name of the process that describes Xing's observations? .... [1]

b) Explain how the smell spread out.

....

....

.... [3]

c) How would Xing's observations be different on a warm summer's day compared to a cold winter's day?

....

....

.... [4]

3 Marlie put a spatula of 1 g ammonium nitrate into 100 g of water and watched as it dissolved.

a) Classify this experiment as a chemical or physical change. Explain your answer.

....

.... [2]

b) Marlie noticed that the temperature dropped on adding the ammonium nitrate to water. What does this tell her about this change?

.... [1]

c) What was the mass of the final solution? .... [1]

d) Describe how Marlie could separate the solution to collect solid ammonium nitrate.

.... [1]

4 Zoe heated 1.2 g of green copper(II) carbonate powder in a boiling tube. She noticed that the powder turned black. The reaction can be represented in a particle diagram.

Key:
○ Copper atoms
● Carbon atoms
○ Oxygen atoms

a) Classify this experiment as a chemical or physical change. Explain your answer.

....

.... [3]

b) Zoe measured 0.8 g of the black copper(II) oxide in the boiling tube at the end of the experiment. What was the mass of carbon dioxide made?

....

.... [2]

c) Write a word equation for this reaction.

.... [2]

5 State whether each of the following statements about the **particle model** are **true** (T) or **false** (F). Write **T** or **F** in the spaces provided.

a) Particles in liquids and gases can flow past each other and take the shape of the container. .... [1]

b) Particles get bigger as they get heated. .... [1]

c) Particles in a solid are in a fixed position and vibrate. .... [1]

d) Gases are usually less dense than solids of the same substance. .... [1]

e) Gas pressure can be increased by increasing the volume of the container. .... [1]

f) Liquids diffuse faster than gases at the same temperature. .... [1]

g) Ice has less energy that the same mass of steam. .... [1]

6 Steph measured a 100 cm length of copper. She heated it and then carefully re-measured it. She found the new length to be 100.17 cm.

a) Use the particle model to explain Steph's observation.

....

....

.... [3]

b) Steph then re-heated the copper to 1086°C, which is 1°C over copper's melting point. In the space below, draw a diagram to show the arrangement of the particles at this temperature.

[2]

Total Marks .... / 38

Working Scientifically

1 Younus decided to measure the density of some different objects. He had 1 cm cubes of iron, brick and lead.

a) What piece of measuring equipment would Younus have used to measure the mass of the cubes?

.... [1]

b) Draw a results table for Younus to record the masses of the different cubes.

[4]

c) Younus found that the iron had a mass of 7.9 g, lead had a mass of 11.3 g and brick had a mass of 1.4 g. Add these data to your results table from part **b)**. [1]

d) The volume of a cube can be calculated by the following:

volume of cube = length of side × width of side × depth of side

Calculate the volume of each of the cubes. Give the unit for your answer.

volume = _____ [2]

2 Alice decided to measure the density of liquid corn syrup. Using a top pan balance, she measured a 13 g sample of corn syrup.

a) What piece of measuring equipment would Alice have used to measure the volume of 13 g of corn syrup?

_____ [1]

b) Alice measured the volume as 10 ml. What is the volume in cm^3?

_____ [2]

c) Density can be calculated by the following:

density = mass ÷ volume

Calculate the density of corn syrup. Give the unit for your answer.

density = _____ [3]

3 Fatima placed some candle wax in a beaker. She slowly heated the beaker and recorded the temperature every minute and plotted the results on a graph. Her results are shown below.

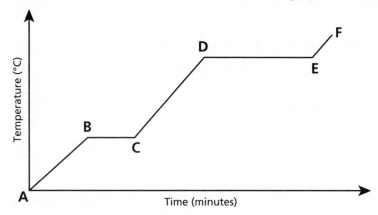

a) What piece of equipment would Fatima have used to measure the temperature?

_____ [1]

b) What is the independent variable? _____ [1]

c) What is the dependent variable? .... [1]

d) Why does Fatima need to be careful with the candle wax?

.... [1]

e) At the end of the experiment, Fatima allowed her equipment to cool. She measured the mass of the equipment and noticed there was a mass loss.

Explain why there was a mass loss.

....

....

....

.... [3]

4 John wanted to make a solution of sodium hydroxide. He measured out 5 g of corrosive sodium hydroxide and added it to 100 cm³ of water.

a) What safety equipment must John wear and why?

....

....

.... [3]

b) What piece of equipment would John make the solution in?

.... [1]

c) Concentration can be calculated by the following:

concentration = mass ÷ volume

Calculate the concentration of sodium hydroxide. Give the unit for your answer.

concentration = ... [3]

Total Marks .... / 28

1 Read the passage about alloys, then answer the questions that follow.

> 1p and 2p coins in the UK are often called coppers, but they aren't made of pure copper. Traditionally they were made from bronze – an alloy comprised of 97% copper, 2.5% tin, and zinc. However, as copper prices rose, bronze became too expensive for this use. So, from 1992, these coins were made of copper-plated steel.

a) What percentage of zinc is there in bronze? .... % [1]

b) What **two** alloys are mentioned in the passage? .... [2]

c) Explain why modern 1p and 2p coins are magnetic but traditional bronze ones are not.

....

....

.... [3]

d) Draw a particle diagram to represent the particles in steel.

[2]

e) Explain why steel is harder than pure iron.

.... [1]

2 Read the passage about water, then answer the questions that follow.

> The water cycle describes how the finite resource of water changes state and circulates around our Earth.

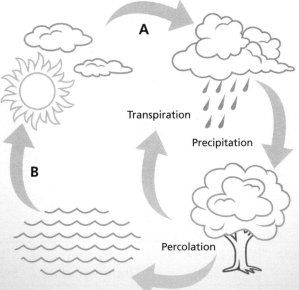

A

Transpiration

Precipitation

B

Percolation

a) Name the state changes shown in letters on the diagram.

   A: .... [1]

   B: .... [1]

b) Are the processes shown in the water cycle a **chemical** or **physical** change?
Explain your answer.

....

....

.... [2]

c) Icebergs are blocks of ice that float on the surface of water.

Explain why icebergs can float on water.

....

....

.... [2]

Total Marks .... / 15

	Vocabulary Builder	Maths Skills	Testing Understanding	Working Scientifically	Science in Use
Total Marks	.... / 19	.... / 31	.... / 38	.... / 28	.... / 15

Chemistry

Explaining Chemical Changes

Vocabulary Builder

1 Match the key word to the description of the type of substance.

Key word	Definition

Key word	**Definition**
Base	A substance that makes a solution with a pH = 7
Neutral	A substance that reacts with an acid that can dissolve in water to make a solution with a pH > 7
Salt	A substance that contains hydrogen and can dissolve in water to make a solution with a pH < 7
Alkali	A substance made in a neutralisation reaction
Acid	A substance that reacts with an acid

[4]

2 Complete the sentences about combustion using the terms from the box. You can use the terms once, more than once or not at all.

hydrocarbons	petrol	energy	natural gas
	burning	force	heat

Combustion reactions involve _____ a fuel with oxygen. The stored

chemical _____ in the fuel is transferred into heat and light energy.

_____ are fuels that contain only hydrogen and carbon. Many everyday

fuels like _____ in cars and _____ used to heat our

homes are hydrocarbon fuels. [5]

3 What is an indicator?

....

.... [2]

4 For each of the following general equations, classify the type of chemical reaction happening. Choose from the terms in the box below. You can use each term once, more than once or not at all.

complete combustion	oxidation	incomplete combustion	neutralisation

a) hydrocarbon + oxygen → carbon dioxide + water .... [1]

b) acid + alkali → salt + water .... [1]

c) calcium + oxygen → calcium oxide .... [1]

d) metal carbonate + acid → salt + carbon dioxide + water .... [1]

e) hydrocarbon + oxygen → carbon dioxide + carbon +
carbon monoxide + water .... [1]

5 What is the name of the medicine that is used to treat indigestion or heartburn?

Tick **one** box.

Antacid ☐ Strong alkali ☐

Inacid ☐ Antiacid ☐ [1]

6 Which of the following statements about **combustion** are **true** (T) and which are **false** (F)?

Write **T** or **F** in the spaces provided.

a) You only need fuel and oxygen for combustion to happen. .... [1]

b) Combustion is an exothermic chemical reaction. .... [1]

c) Hydrogen gas can be used as a fuel for rockets. .... [1]

d) Carbon monoxide is a greenhouse gas. .... [1]

e) Soot is made from the incomplete combustion of hydrocarbon fuels. .... [1]

Total Marks .... / 22

Maths Skills

1   Sunil wanted to investigate the reaction between marble chips and hydrochloric acid to make a salt, water and carbon dioxide gas. He measured out 0.01 kg of marble chips and put it into 50 cm³ of dilute hydrochloric acid in a conical flask. He then monitored the mass of the reaction on a top-pan balance.

The graph of Sunil's results is shown below.

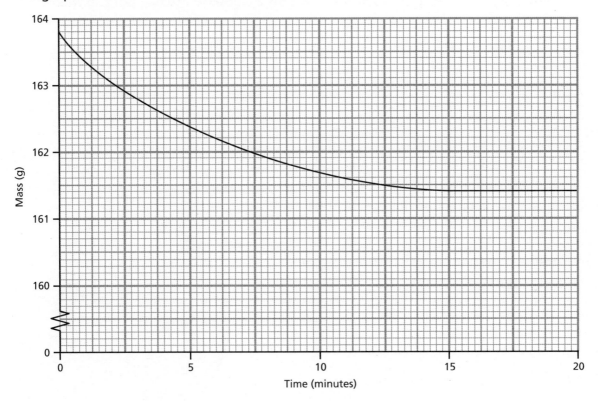

a) What was the starting mass of the whole experiment? .... [1]

b) What was the mass of carbon dioxide released to the atmosphere?

mass = ... [2]

c) How many seconds did Sunil monitor the experiment for?

seconds = ... [2]

d) In grams, what was the mass of marble that Sunil used?

mass = ... g [2]

2 The pH scale measures acidity and is a special scale where an increase of 1 pH unit has a ten times difference in acidity. So, in a solution with pH 1, the acidity level is 10 times greater than in pH 2, and 100 times greater than in pH 3.

How many times more acidic is a solution with pH 2 compared to each of the following?

a) pH 3 .... [1]

b) pH 4 .... [1]

c) pH 5 .... [1]

d) pH 6 .... [1]

3 About twenty-eight million tonnes of nitric acid are made in the world each year. The pie chart shows the main industrial uses of this useful chemical.

a) Write the mass of nitric acid made per year as a number.

Uses of Nitric Acid

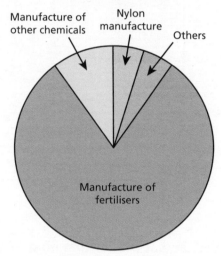
Manufacture of other chemicals

Nylon manufacture

Others

Manufacture of fertilisers

mass = ... tonnes [1]

b) What is the biggest use of nitric acid?

.... [1]

c) 10% of the nitric acid produced is used to make other chemicals. What is the mass of the nitric acid used to make the other chemicals? Give your answer in standard form.

mass = ... tonnes [3]

d) What percentage of nitric acid is used in nylon manufacture?

.... % [1]

Total Marks .... / 17

1 Complete the table below to show the names of the salts that are made when different acids react with bases. [4]

Name of acid	Name of salt	Example
Hydrochloric acid	c) _____	Sodium chloride
a) _____	Sulfate	Copper sulfate
b) _____	d) _____	Magnesium nitrate

2 Complete the word equations by writing the names of the missing substances.

a) calcium + _____ → calcium oxide

b) ethanol + oxygen → _____ + carbon dioxide

c) _____ + hydrochloric acid → magnesium chloride + hydrogen

d) sodium carbonate + _____ → carbon dioxide + water + sodium chloride

e) potassium hydroxide + sulfuric acid → _____ + _____ [6]

3 The fire triangle can be useful in helping to make predictions about what is needed for combustion to happen.

a) Complete the labels on the fire triangle diagram. [2]

A: _____ B: _____

Fuel

b) Write a word equation for the complete combustion of the hydrocarbon methane.

_____ [2]

c) Write a word equation for the incomplete combustion of the hydrocarbon methane.

_____ [2]

d) Draw lines to match up the pollutants from combustion with the problems that they can cause.

Pollutant

Soot (carbon)

Carbon monoxide

Sulfur dioxide and nitrogen oxides

Carbon dioxide

Problem

A greenhouse gas linked to climate change

A toxic gas that can lead to poisoning and death

An irritant that can cause breathing difficulties

Acidic gases that cause acid rain

[3]

4 Acids react with bases to make a salt and other products.

a) Complete the general word equations for the reactions of acids with bases.

i) metal + acid → .... + ... [2]

ii) metal carbonate + acid → .... + ... + ... [3]

iii) metal hydroxide + acid → .... + ... [2]

iv) metal oxide + acid → .... + ... [2]

b) In some reactions a gas is made. The gas can be collected and tested to show which gas was made.

i) Describe how to test for hydrogen gas.

....

.... [2]

ii) Describe how to test for carbon dioxide gas.

....

....

.... [3]

5 A student wanted to investigate what happened when they mixed sodium carbonate solution with hydrochloric acid to make carbon dioxide, water and sodium chloride. They added universal indicator to both solutions and mixed exactly 10 cm³ of each solution into a conical flask and observed bubbles and fizzing which stopped after about 10 seconds.

a) Write a word equation for the reaction that the student was observing.

_____ [2]

b) On adding the universal indicator, what colour would the following solutions have been?

i) Hydrochloric acid _____ [1]

ii) Sodium carbonate _____ [1]

iii) The solution at the end of the experiment _____ [1]

c) Why did the pupil observe bubbles and fizzing?

_____ [1]

d) What type of chemical reaction was the pupil investigating?

_____ [1]

Total Marks _____ / 40

Working Scientifically

1 Jesse wanted to investigate how the mass changed as marble chips reacted with hydrochloric acid. A diagram of the equipment that he used is shown below.

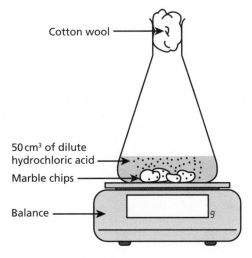

Cotton wool

50 cm³ of dilute hydrochloric acid

Marble chips

Balance

a) What piece of equipment would Jesse have used to measure the volume of hydrochloric acid?

_____ [1]

b) What is the name of the equipment that Jesse used to hold the chemical reaction?

_____ [1]

Video Solution

P47, Q3a)-b)

c) Why did Jesse use a piece of cotton wool in his experiment?

.... [1]

d) What is the dependent variable in this experiment? .... [1]

e) Predict and explain what you think will happen to the mass in this experiment.

....

....

.... [4]

2 Daiyu put some universal indicator into different samples of liquids. She recorded her results on the pH chart below.

pH	0	1	2	3	4	5	6	7	8	9	10	11	12	13	14
Colour	Red			Orange		Yellow		Green	Dark green		Blue		Indigo–violet		

Labels above chart: Lemon juice (pH 2), Cola (pH 3), Tomato juice (pH 4), Water (pH 7), Baking soda (pH 9)

a) Describe how Daiyu would use universal indicator to get her results.

....

....

.... [4]

b) Draw and complete a results table for Daiyu's observations.

[2]

3 Premal wanted to investigate which antacid would be the best to cure heartburn. She added universal indicator to a beaker of hydrochloric acid and added the recommended dose of each antacid to the acid.

a) What observations could Premal make to help her decide which is the best antacid?

_____ [2]

b) How would Premal make sure that this is a fair test?

_____

_____

_____ [3]

c) What safety precautions should Premal take when completing this investigation?

_____ [2]

d) Why would litmus not be a useful indicator to use in this experiment?

_____

_____ [2]

Total Marks _____ / 23

Science in Use

1 Read the passage about farming then answer the questions that follow.

Different crops grow best in different soil pH values, so farmers may need to add substances to change the pH of soils to improve the yield and quality of their crops. For example, calcium oxide is an insoluble white solid that is more commonly known as lime. Farmers add lime to the soil to increase the pH of soils.

a) What type of substance is calcium oxide? _____ [1]

b) What type of chemical reaction happens between acids in the soil and lime? _____ [1]

c) What indicator could the farmer use to test the pH of their soil?

_____ [1]

d) What piece of equipment could the farmer use to test the pH of their soil?

_____ [1]

e) Lime can react with water to make only calcium hydroxide or slaked lime.

Write a word equation for this reaction.

.... [2]

f) Slaked lime can dissolve in water to make limewater with a pH of 12.4

What type of substance is limewater? .... [1]

2 Read the passage about **combustion** in the home then answer the questions that follow.

Natural gas is mainly methane (CH_4) and used as a fuel to heat our homes and cook our foods. The hydrocarbon fuel is combusted in boilers, on cooker hobs and in ovens to transfer stored chemical energy to thermal energy. Natural gas has no smell but a harmless smelly gas called methanethiol is added to the gas supply.

It is important that the gas appliances are serviced regularly to make sure that they are working efficiently.

a) Why can methane be described as a hydrocarbon?

.... [2]

b) What gas from the air is needed to combust methane?

.... [1]

c) Some faulty boilers have black powder on the wall near them.

Describe how this black powder could have been made from the boiler and explain why this is a serious concern.

....

....

....

.... [4]

Total Marks .... / 14

	Vocabulary Builder	Maths Skills	Testing Understanding	Working Scientifically	Science in Use
Total Marks	/ 22	/ 17	/ 40	/ 23	/ 14

1 The box contains examples of forces.

friction	magnetic	aerodynamic lift	gravity
tension	weight	air resistance	drag	electric

a) Select **three** contact forces from the box.

.... [3]

b) Select **three** non-contact forces from the box.

.... [3]

2 A force is either **attractive** or **repulsive**. Identify which interactions are attractive and which are repulsive.

a) Two magnets placed near to each other with north poles facing .... [1]

b) A ball falling towards the ground .... [1]

c) A positively charged balloon placed near to another positively charged balloon .... [1]

3 The space around an object that exerts a non-contact force on another object is called a **field.**

Complete the sentences using words from this box:

gravitational	magnetic	electric

a) An object falls to the ground because of the Earth's .... field. [1]

b) Small bits of paper jump up to a charged plastic ruler because of the

ruler's .... field. [1]

c) A satellite follows a circular path because of the Earth's .... field. [1]

d) The needle of a compass points in the direction of north because of

the Earth's .... field. [1]

4 When an inflated balloon is rubbed with a cloth it can become electrically charged.

Which particles are involved with the transfer of electrical charge? Tick **one** box.

molecule ☐   proton ☐   electron ☐   [1]

5 Which one of the materials can be described as a magnetic material? Tick **one** box.

iron ☐   aluminium ☐   polythene ☐   [1]

6 The diagram shows a plastic water bottle with three holes of equal size.

a) Which jet of water is being pushed out of the bottle with the greatest force? Tick **one** box.

top ☐

middle ☐

bottom ☐ [1]

b) What does this tell us about the pressure in a liquid?

.... [1]

7 The diagram shows a solid sphere that has just been submerged and released in a tank of water.

The arrows represent the force exerted by the water on the surface of the sphere.

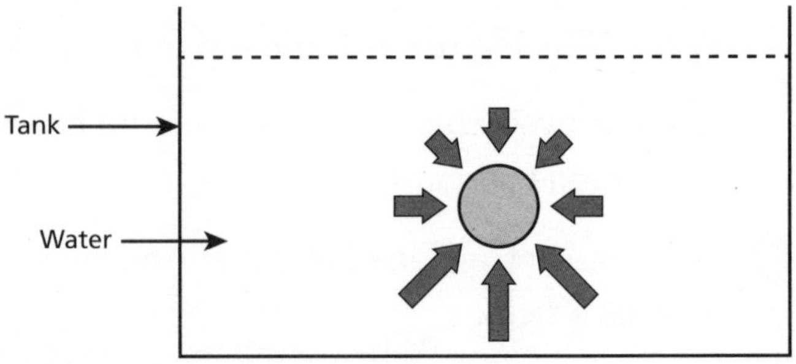

Tank →

Water →

For the following questions, tick **one** box.

a) What direction is the overall force on the sphere due to the liquid?   [1]

left ☐   right ☐   up ☐   down ☐

b) What is the name given to the force exerted by a liquid on a submerged object?   [1]

friction ☐   upthrust ☐   downthrust ☐   displacement ☐

8 The pressure exerted by air molecules on the surface of an object is called atmospheric pressure. Read the sentences and write down if each one is **true** or **false**.

a) As you climb a mountain the weight of the air above you increases.   .... [1]

b) Atmospheric pressure decreases as height increases.   .... [1]

c) Atmospheric pressure at sea level is greater than at the top of a mountain.

.... [1]

Total Marks .... / 22

Maths Skills

1 The force of gravity acting on an object is also known as the object's weight. The force of gravity on a 1 kg mass on the Earth is 10 N.

Calculate the weight of a 3 kg mass.

weight = ... N [1]

2 The strength of the Earth's gravitational field is 10 N/kg.

a) Calculate the force of gravity on a mass of 5 kg.

force = ... N [1]

b) A bag of potatoes with a mass of 2 kg is placed on a table.

Calculate the force exerted by the bag on the surface of the table.

force = ... N [1]

3 The diagram shows the width and length measurements of a box.

a) The box is placed on the floor. Calculate the area of the box in contact with the floor.

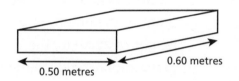

0.50 metres

0.60 metres

area = ... m² [1]

b) The weight of the box is 30 N. Use the formula below, and your answer to part a), to calculate the pressure exerted by the box on the floor.

pressure = force ÷ area

pressure = ... N/m² [1]

4 A man has a mass of 70 kg. The Earth's gravitational field strength is 10 N/kg.

a) Calculate the force exerted by the man standing on the floor.

force = ... N [1]

b) The total area of the man's shoes is 0.07 m². Use the formula below, and your answer to part a), to calculate the pressure exerted by the man on the floor when he is standing on both feet.

pressure = force ÷ area

pressure = ... N/m² [1]

c) Calculate the pressure the man would exert on the floor if he stood on one foot.

pressure = ... N/m² [1]

5 At sea level the Earth's atmosphere exerts a force of 100 000 N on an area of 1 m². The average surface area of an adult is 2 m².

What is the total force exerted by the atmosphere on an adult?

force = _____ N   [1]

6 Asana has plotted data points on the graph to show how the Earth's gravitational field changes at different heights above the Earth's surface.

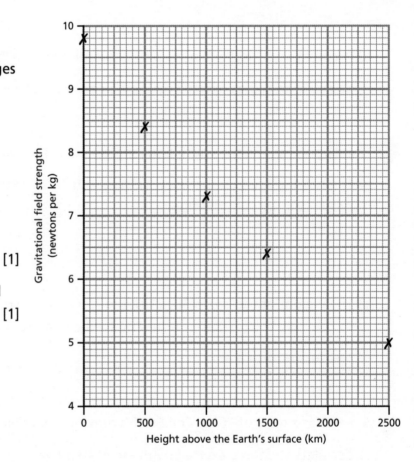

a) One point has not been plotted. Add the following point to the graph: At a height of 2000 km, the gravitational field strength is 5.7 N per kg.   [1]

b) Draw a single smooth curved line through the points.   [1]

c) The International Space Station orbits at a height of about 400 km above the Earth's surface. Use Asana's graph to answer the following question:

What would be a good estimate of the Earth's gravitational field 400 km above the Earth's surface in N per kg? Tick **one** box.

between 7.7 and 8.0 ☐   between 8.1 and 8.4 ☐   between 8.5 and 8.8 ☐   [1]

d) What other gravitational field might affect the motion of a spacecraft travelling through the Solar System?

_____   [1]

Total Marks _____ / 13

1 The diagram shows a container that has been placed on a table.

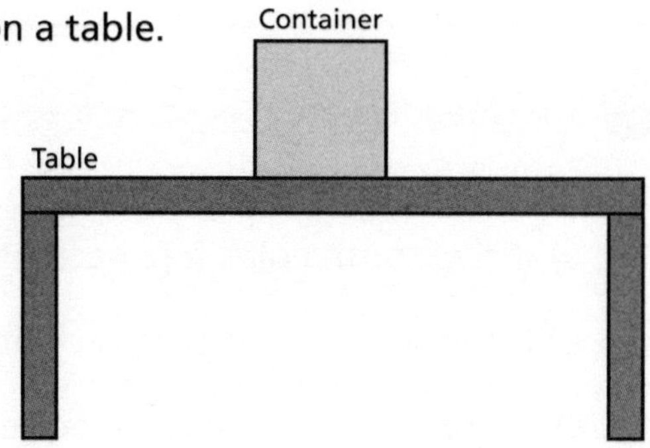

a) Draw an arrow from the centre of the container to represent the force of gravity exerted on the container by the Earth. [1]

Container

Table

b) The mass of the container is 2.5 kg. The strength of the gravitational field at the Earth's surface is about 10 N/kg.

What gravitational force does the Earth exert on the container? Tick **one** box. [1]

2.5 N ☐   25 N ☐   250 N ☐

c) The container is stationary, so the overall force on it must be zero. Read the sentences and write down if each one is **true** or **false**.

i) The table exerts an upward force on the container. _____ [1]

ii) The force exerted by the table on the container is a non-contact force. _____ [1]

iii)The force exerted by the table on the container is equal to the container's weight.

_____ [1]

2 A child has a mass of 30 kg. The child is standing on the floor. Determine the size and direction of the force exerted by the floor on the child. (Earth's gravitational field is 10 N/kg.)

force = _____ N [1]

direction: _____ [1]

3 The speed of a falling object is measured at two points in its path. Part way through its fall its speed is measured as 10 m/s. Just before hitting the ground its speed is 14 m/s. Read the sentences and write down if each one is **true** or **false**.

a) The object is accelerating. _____ [1]

b) The object has a constant speed. _____ [1]

c) The air resistance on the object is greater than its weight. _____ [1]

d) The kinetic energy of the object is increasing as it falls. _____ [1]

4 Two magnets are placed near to each other. Use the words **attractive** or **repulsive** to complete the sentences.

   a) If two south poles face each other, the force between them is .... [1]

   b) If two north poles face each other, the force between them is .... [1]

   c) If north and south poles face each other, the force between them is .... [1]

5 The diagram shows two electrically charged rods, labelled A and B. Moving rod B towards rod A causes rod A to move away. The charge on rod B is positive.

   State whether the charge on rod A is positive or negative and explain your answer.

   Stand   A   B

   ....

   ....

   ....

   .... [3]

6 When a polythene rod is rubbed with a cloth it becomes negatively charged.

   a) What particles have been transferred from the cloth to the rod? .... [1]

   b) What type of field is created by a charged polythene rod? .... [1]

   c) How is the cloth affected by the process of charging the polythene rod?

   .... [1]

7 The space around the Earth acts as gravitational field, a magnetic field, and in some locations, a temporary electric field. Read the sentences and write down if each one is **true** or **false**.

   a) The gravitational field causes objects to fall towards the Earth's surface. .... [1]

   b) The magnetic field can be used by aircraft pilots to determine the height of the aircraft above the ground. .... [1]

   c) The electric field can cause lightning strikes. .... [1]

8 A teacher demonstrates the effects of liquid pressure using the two cans shown on the right.

The cans contain holes that water jets are forced through.

(Note: the apparatus that keeps the cans full of water is not shown in the diagram.)

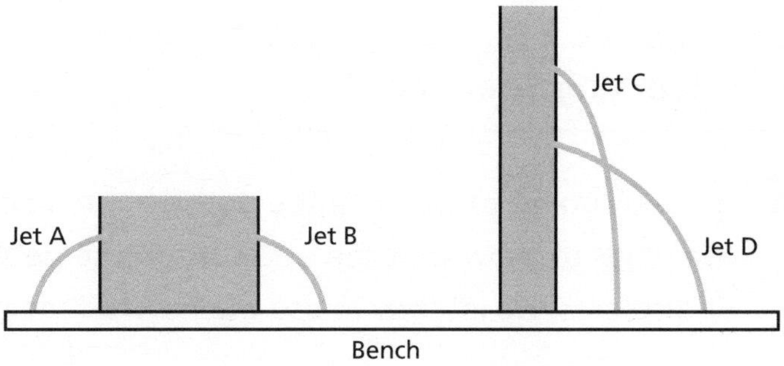

Jet C

Jet A   Jet B   Jet D

Bench

a) Explain which water jets show that liquid pressure is larger at a greater depth.

....

.... [2]

b) Explain which water jets show that liquid pressure has the same value in all directions at the same depth.

....

.... [2]

9 The diagram shows an object that has just been placed on the water's surface.

The arrows on the diagram represent the forces acting on the object caused by liquid pressure.

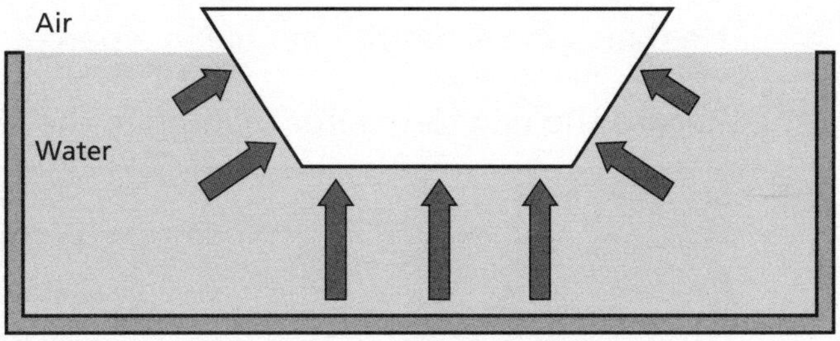

Air

Water

a) What feature of the diagram is used to show that liquid pressure increases at greater depths?

.... [1]

b) Complete the sentence using words from the box.

weight	upthrust

The object will sink if the .... is smaller than the .... [1]

Total Marks .... / 29

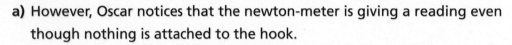

Working Scientifically

1 Oscar is going to measure the upthrust on a pebble immersed in water. He plans to show that the upthrust on the pebble is equal to the weight of water it displaces. He intends to use the newton-meter shown opposite.

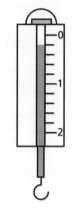

a) However, Oscar notices that the newton-meter is giving a reading even though nothing is attached to the hook.

He adjusts the screw at the top of the newton-meter so that it reads zero when nothing is attached to the hook.

Explain why it is important that he makes this adjustment.

_____

_____ **[1]**

b) Oscar attaches the pebble to the hook with nylon thread. He records the weight of the pebble as 1.6 N in the table below.

He then submerges the pebble in a pan of water.

Record the newton-meter reading in the table below. **[1]**

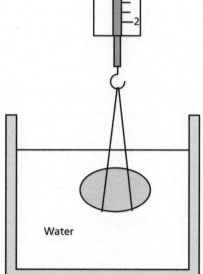

Weight of pebble (newtons)	Newton-meter reading when pebble is submerged (newtons)	Upthrust acting on the pebble (newtons)
1.6		

c) Determine the upthrust acting on the pebble and record this value in the table above. **[1]**

d) Explain what causes the upthrust on the pebble.

_____

_____

_____

_____ **[2]**

Water

e) Oscar uses the apparatus shown on the right to measure the volume of water displaced by the pebble.

Give the name of the pieces of apparatus labelled A and B.

A: _____ [1]

B: _____ [1]

f) A volume of 61 cm³ of water is displaced when the pebble is submerged in the water. A volume of 1 cm³ of water has a weight of 0.0098 N.

Calculate the weight of water displaced by the pebble.

weight = _____ N   [1]

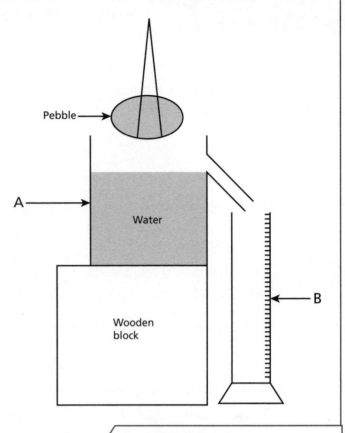

Pebble

A →

Water

Wooden block

← B

Total Marks _____ / 8

1 Read the passage and answer the questions that follow.

Whether you are flying an aircraft, skydiving or climbing a mountain, it is useful to know your distance above sea level. This distance is known as your altitude. The device that gives you this information is called an altimeter. In this image, one skydiver has a wrist mounted altimeter, and the other has an altimeter attached to the back of his hand.

Inside an altimeter is a device that measures the pressure of the surrounding air, known as the atmospheric pressure. Scientists have discovered that the value of atmospheric pressure decreases as altitude increases. The data table below gives some values for atmospheric pressure at various heights above sea level.

Altitude (metres)	0 (sea level)	1000	2000	3000	4000	5000	6000	7000	8000
Atmospheric pressure (kN/m²)	101	88	76	66	57	50	43	37	32

a) Explain why the atmosphere exerts its greatest force on your body when you are at sea level.

_____ [1]

b) Most skydivers jump from an aircraft at an altitude of 4200 m.

Use the data table to predict the atmospheric pressure at this altitude.

atmospheric pressure = _____ kN/m² [1]

c) A skydiver falls freely for about 1 minute before reaching a maximum constant speed of 190 km/h (about 120 mph).

At this speed, what upward force is balancing the skydiver's weight?

_____ [1]

d) The wrist-mounted altimeter measures the atmospheric pressure, and its electronic circuits convert this to the corresponding height above sea level.

Suggest why skydivers use their altimeters to keep track of their altitude as they fall.

_____ [1]

e) Some very experienced skydivers jump from an aircraft at an altitude of 5500 m. This gives them an extra 20 seconds of freefall to practise their moves. However, at this altitude a skydiver requires a cylinder of oxygen and a breathing mask.

Suggest why this additional supply of oxygen is required.

_____ [1]

f) A mountaineer uses his altimeter in connection with a map, showing heights above sea level, to pinpoint his position.

Use the data table to predict the value of atmospheric pressure at the summit of Mount Everest. The altitude at the summit is 8849 metres.

atmospheric pressure = _____ [1]

Total Marks _____ / 6

	Vocabulary Builder	Maths Skills	Testing Understanding	Working Scientifically	Science in Use
Total Marks	_____ / 22	_____ / 13	_____ / 29	_____ / 8	_____ / 6

Vocabulary Builder

1 The box below contains the names of some materials.

| iron | polythene | copper | aluminium | PVC | steel | polystyrene |

Select a material from the box to fill in the blank space in each of the following sentences.

a) .... is a good conductor of electricity. [1]

b) .... is a good electrical insulator. [1]

c) .... can be used to coat electrical cables. [1]

d) .... can be used to make a permanent magnet. [1]

e) .... is used to make an electromagnet. [1]

2 Waheed magnetises a steel nail by repeatedly stroking the nail with a permanent magnet. The arrows on the diagram show the direction that the magnet should be moved.

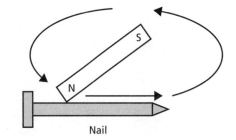

Nail

a) Describe how Waheed could use iron filings to test the nail to see if it has been magnetised.

.... [1]

b) Describe how Waheed could use a plotting compass to test the nail to see if it has been magnetised.

....

.... [1]

3 The diagram on the right shows the electric circuit for a torch, with components labelled A, B, C and D.

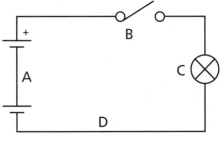

a) Give the names of the components. The first one has been done for you.

A: .... *battery* ....

B: .... [1]

C: .... [1]

D: .... [1]

b) Complete the sentences about the operation of the torch. Use terms from the box below.

potential difference	resistance	light
chemical	kinetic	current	power

i) When the switch is closed, the lamp transfers .... energy stored in the

battery to .... energy. **[2]**

ii) The lamp's opposition to the flow of electric current is called .... **[1]**

iii) The battery creates the .... needed to force the electric current

through the lamp. **[1]**

4 The diagram below includes a device for measuring the electric current in the circuit.

a) Give the name of the current measuring device. .... **[1]**

b) In the space alongside the diagram, draw the matching circuit diagram using the correct
circuit symbols.

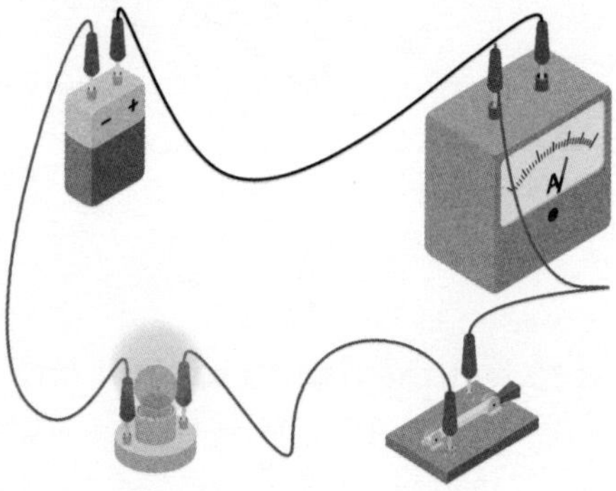

[4]

c) Give the name of a device that could be used to measure
the potential difference across the lamp. .... **[1]**

d) Which unit is used for the electrical resistance of the lamp? Tick **one** box.

amp ☐

ohm ☐

volt ☐ **[1]**

Total Marks .... / 21

1 The circuit below includes a lamp connected to a battery.

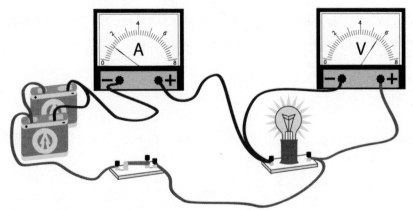

a) Give the potential difference reading with its unit.

potential difference = ... [2]

b) Give the electric current reading with its unit.

electric current = ... [2]

c) Use the formula below to calculate the lamp's resistance in ohms.

resistance = potential difference ÷ electric current

resistance = ... ohm [1]

2 The image shown is a typical LED bulb that can be bought to use at home.

To light fully, this type of bulb needs a potential difference of 230 V.
The table shows three LED bulbs with different power ratings.

Bulb	Potential difference (volts)	Power rating (watts)
X	230	5
Y	230	8
Z	230	10

a) Which bulb is the brightest? Tick **one** box.

X ☐   Y ☐   Z ☐   [1]

b) Which bulb would cost the least if switched on for one hour? Tick **one** box.

X ☐   Y ☐   Z ☐   [1]

Magnetism and Electricity

3 An LED light bulb has a power rating of 10 watts. This means that the bulb transfers 10 joules of electrical energy to light energy every second.

a) How many seconds are there in 1 hour?

.... s [1]

b) If the bulb is switched on for 1 hour, how much energy does it transfer?

energy = ... J [1]

c) The cost of 200 000 J of electrical energy is about 1 pence.

What is the cost of the 10-watt bulb being switched on for 1 hour? Tick **one** box.

less than 1 pence ☐   between 1 and 10 pence ☐   more than 10 pence ☐ [1]

4 An electric heater operates at a power of 2000 watts.

a) Complete the sentence:

The heater transfers 2000 joules of .... energy to .... energy in 1 second.
[2]

b) How much energy does the heater transfer if it is switched on for 1 hour?

energy = ... J [1]

5 The table below contains incomplete information about some household electrical appliances.

a) Fill in the missing data. [4]

Appliance	Required potential difference (volts)	Power (watts)	Power (kilowatts)	Electric current (amps)	Resistance (ohms)
kettle	230	i)	2.3	10	23
vacuum cleaner	230	920	0.92	4	iii) ....
food mixer	230	1150	ii)	5	46
freezer	230	230	0.23	1	iv) ....

b) Which appliance costs the most to run for 1 minute? .... [1]

Total Marks .... / 18

1 The diagram represents the
Earth's magnetic field.

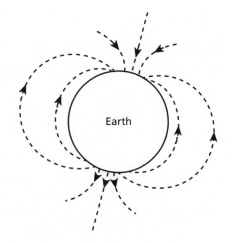

a) What type of magnet has a similar shaped
field as the Earth? .... [1]

b) Name the device that can determine the
direction of the Earth's magnetic field. .... [1]

c) Give an example of an application of the
device named in part **b)**. .... [1]

2 The diagram below shows four circuits labelled W, X, Y and Z.

       W   **X**   **Y**   **Z**

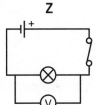

For each of the following questions, tick **one** box.

a) Which circuit contains a battery of two cells?

  W ☐   X ☐   Y ☐   Z ☐   [1]

b) Which circuit contains two lamps connected in series?

  W ☐   X ☐   Y ☐   Z ☐   [1]

c) Which circuit contains two lamps connected in parallel?

  W ☐   X ☐   Y ☐   Z ☐   [1]

d) Which circuit contains a device for measuring the electric current flowing
through a lamp?

  W ☐   X ☐   Y ☐   Z ☐   [1]

e) Which circuit contains a device for measuring potential difference?

  W ☐   X ☐   Y ☐   Z ☐   [1]

3 Diagram 1 shows a nail wrapped with conducting wire connected to a cell. The switch is open and all four plotting compass needles point in a northerly direction.

Diagram 1

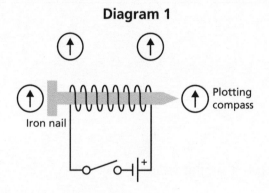

Diagram 2 shows the same apparatus but now the switch has been closed.

Diagram 2

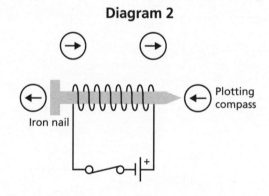

a) Explain why the plotting compass needles changed direction when the switch was closed.

....

.... [2]

b) Diagram 3 shows the effect that a bar magnet has on a plotting compass.

Use diagram 3 to predict which end of the iron nail above acts like a south pole. Explain your answer.

Diagram 3

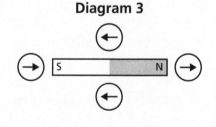

....

....

.... [2]

c) If the switch in the circuit in Diagram 2 was opened, what would happen to the plotting compass needles?

.... [1]

4. The circuit shown contains one lamp and two ammeters – A_1 and A_2. These ammeters measure the size of the electric current at different points in the circuit.

Ammeter A_1 reads 0.06 A.

What is the reading on ammeter A_2? Tick **one** box.

0.04 A ☐   0.06 A ☐   0.08 A ☐   0.12 A ☐   [1]

5. The circuit shown contains two lamps and three ammeters – A_1, A_2 and A_3.

Ammeter A_1 reads 0.10 A. Ammeter A_2 reads 0.05 A.

What is the reading on ammeter A_3? Tick **one** box.

0.05 A ☐   0.10 A ☐   0.15 A ☐   0.20 A ☐   [1]

6. The circuit shown contains two lamps and three ammeters – A_1, A_2 and A_3.

Ammeter A_1 reads 0.025 A. Ammeter A_2 reads 0.025 A.

What is the reading on ammeter A_3? Tick **one** box.

0.015 A ☐   0.025 A ☐   0.04 A ☐   0.05 A ☐   [1]

7. The circuit below contains three lamps and four switches.

State which switches should be closed (on) so that only lamp Y lights. .... [1]

8. Look at the circuit diagram below. Add an arrow at the locations marked with a * to show the current direction in the wire. The first one has been done for you.   [3]

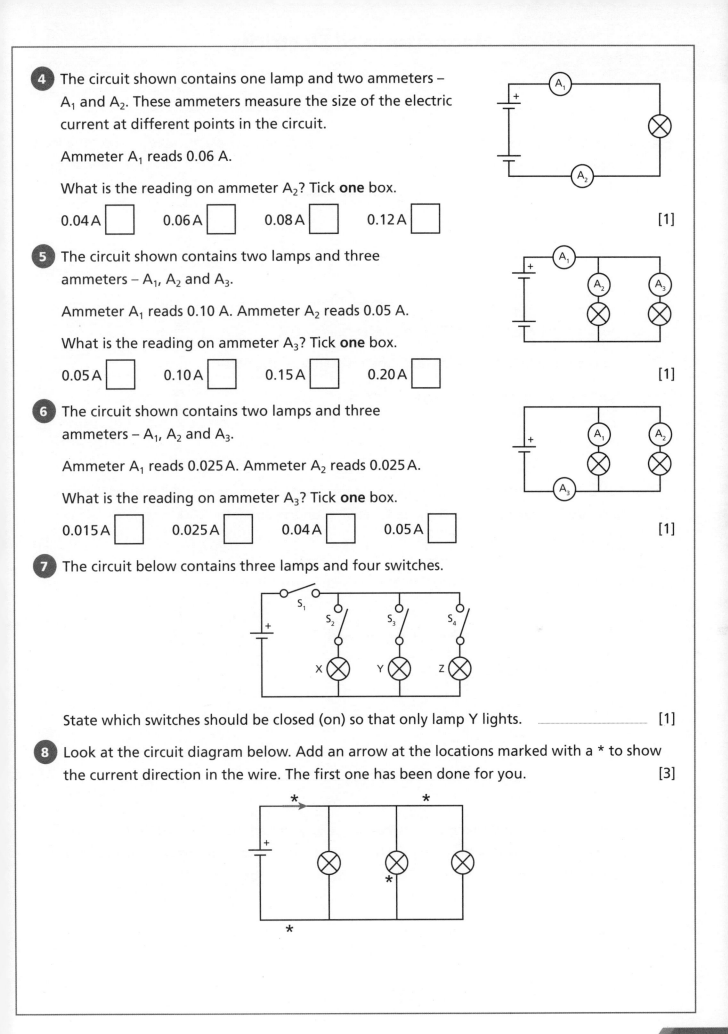

9 Ava constructs the circuit shown below so she can measure the electrical resistance of a long piece of wire.

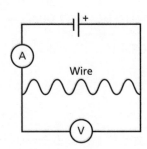

Wire

a) The ammeter reads 0.10 A. The voltmeter reads 2.0 V.

Use the formula below to calculate the resistance of the wire.

resistance = potential difference ÷ current

resistance = ... ohms   [1]

b) Ava cuts the wire in half. This means that the resistance in the circuit is half of the value calculated in part **a)**. What is the new reading on the ammeter? Tick **one** box.

0.05 A ☐   0.10 A ☐   0.15 A ☐   0.20 A ☐   [1]

10 Resistors are used to control the size of the electric current in a circuit.

3-volt battery

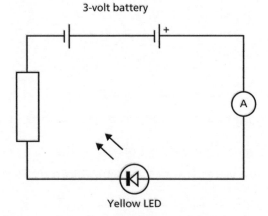

Yellow LED

The circuit shows an LED that gives out a bright yellow light. If the LED had been connected directly across the 3-volt battery it would have burnt out immediately. However, the resistor in the circuit shown protects the LED by controlling the size of the current flowing.

a) To protect the LED, the resistor must have a potential difference of 1.2 V across it and a current of 0.020 A through it.

Calculate the resistance of the resistor in the circuit using the formula below:

resistance = potential difference ÷ current

resistance = _____ ohms [1]

b) Shari calculates that she needs a 30-ohm resistor in the circuit she is building. However, she only has access to resistors of resistance 10 ohm. She can make a 30-ohm resistance by connecting three 10-ohm resistors in series.

In the space below draw three 10-ohm resistors connected in series between terminals X and Y. [1]

X ○

Y ○

11 The circuits, X and Y below, contain two identical resistors, each of resistance 100 ohm.

Circuit X

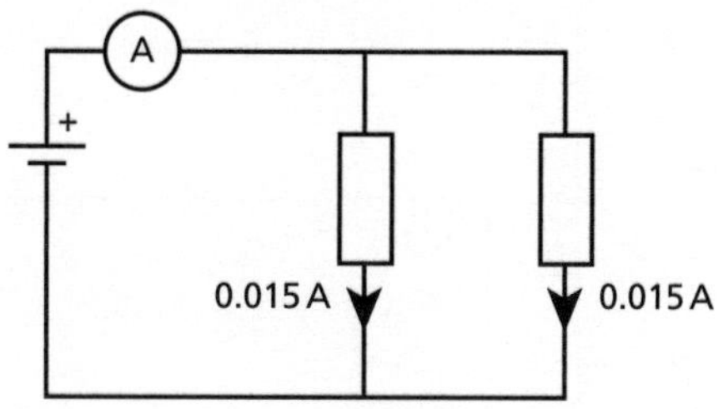

Circuit Y

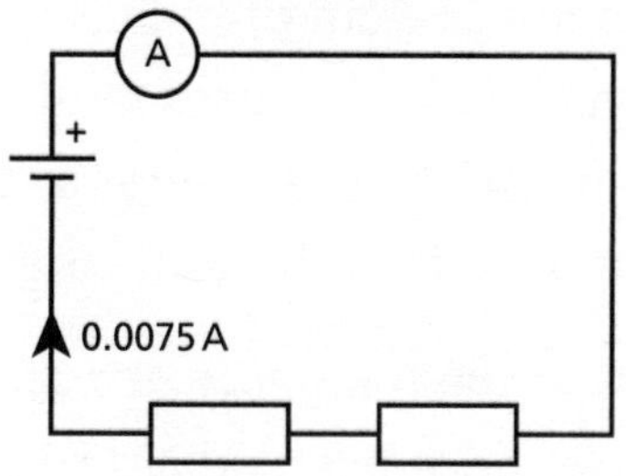

0.015 A   0.015 A   0.0075 A

a) What is the current reading on the ammeter in circuit X? Tick **one** box.

0.0075 A ☐   0.015 A ☐   0.0025 A ☐   0.030 A ☐   [1]

b) What is the current reading on the ammeter in circuit Y? Tick **one** box.

0.0075 A ☐   0.015 A ☐   0.0025 A ☐   0.030 A ☐   [1]

c) Which combination of the 100-ohm resistors, circuit X or circuit Y, creates the greatest opposition to the flow of electric current? Explain your answer.

_____

_____ [2]

Total Marks _____ / 28

> **Working Scientifically**

1 The diagram shows an iron core around which a long piece of wire has been wrapped.

The wire is connected to a battery.

When the switch is closed, the electric current in the wire magnetises the iron core.

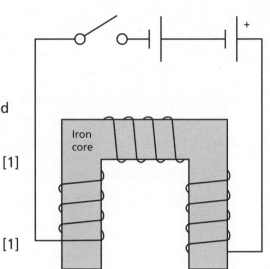

a) What is the name given to an iron core magnetised by an electric current?

.... [1]

b) What happens to the magnetism in the iron core when the switch is opened?

.... [1]

c) Noah wants to measure the strength of the magnetised iron core. He places an iron plate across the bottom of the core and attaches a hanger and masses, as shown. Noah adds masses to the hanger until the iron plate is pulled off the iron core.

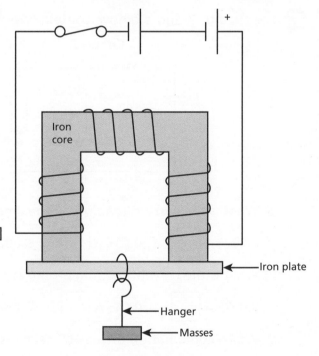

i) The mass of the hanger is 20 g and five 50 g masses have been added to it. Calculate the mass attached to the iron plate.

mass = ... g   [1]

ii) The mass of the iron plate is 30 g. Calculate the total mass in kilograms needed to pull the iron plate away from the iron core.

total mass = ... kg   [1]

iii) Calculate the weight needed to pull the iron plate away from the magnetised iron core by multiplying the total mass in kilograms by gravitational field strength, which is 10 N/kg.

weight = ... N   [1]

d) Noah decides to use the apparatus to investigate if the number of turns of wire wrapped around the iron core affects the strength of the magnetism produced. His data is shown in the table below.

Complete the last two columns in the table.

Number of turns on the iron core	Mass of hanger (grams)	Mass put on hanger (grams)	Mass of iron plate (grams)	Total mass (kilograms)	Total weight needed to pull the plate off the core (newtons)
25	20	250	30		
20	20	190	30		
15	20	130	30		
10	20	70	30		
5	20	10	30		

[5]

e) On the grid below, plot the total weight needed to pull the plate off the core on the *y*-axis against the number of turns on the iron core on the *x*-axis. [5]

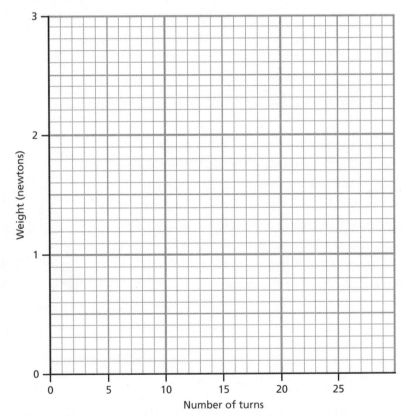

Weight (newtons) vs Number of turns

f) Using a ruler and pencil, draw a straight line through the points you have just plotted. [1]

g) Use the graph to predict what weight would be needed to pull off the iron plate if there were 18 turns on the iron core.

weight = _____ N [1]

h) Whilst Noah was changing the number of turns wrapped around the iron core, he did not change the full length of the wire. This was because he wanted to keep the electric current constant.

Draw a line from each quantity to the type of variable it matches. [2]

Quantity

Electric current

Number of turns

Weight

Variable

Independent variable

Dependent variable

Control variable

Total Marks _____ / 19

Science in Use

1 Read the passage below and answer the questions that follow.

Almost all homes in the UK have a washing machine. Each machine typically completes around 270 washes each year. The drum of the washing machine, containing the clothes to be washed, has to be able to rotate at different speeds. In spin mode, the drum completes typically 1200 revolutions per minute. Driving this rotation is an electric motor like the one shown. A belt links the motor's axle to a pulley attached to the back of the drum.

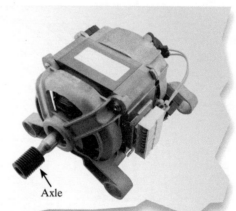

Axle

a) i) Typically, how many washes does a washing machine complete each week?

_____ [1]

ii) In spin mode, how many rotations does the drum complete in one second?

_____ [1]

b) i) Name **two** other houshold appliances that use an electric motor to produce rotation.

_____ [2]

ii) Name **two** forms of transport, not including an electric car, that are driven by an electric motor.

_____ [2]

c) The diagram shows a simplified view of an electric motor. The electricity supply to the coil is not shown in the diagram. The axle is attached to the coil.

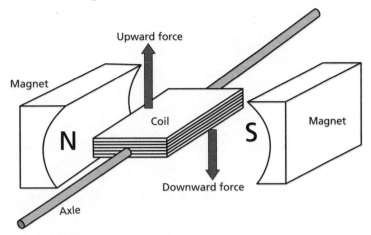

Upward force

Magnet

Coil

N   S   Magnet

Downward force

Axle

Use the words in the box to complete the sentences describing the operation of the motor.

| clockwise | anticlockwise | current | magnetic | coil | electric |

i) When the motor is connected to an electricity supply, the _____ carries an electric current. [1]

ii) This _____ current creates a _____ field which interacts with the magnetic field created by the magnets. [2]

iii) This interaction creates an upward force on one side of the coil and a downward force on the other, making the coil rotate in a _____ direction. [1]

d) An electric car contains a motor that is driven by battery, which requires charging.

Suggest **one** advantage of an electric car.

_____

_____

_____ [1]

Total Marks _____ / 11

	Vocabulary Builder	Maths Skills	Testing Understanding	Working Scientifically	Science in Use
Total Marks	_____ / 21	_____ / 18	_____ / 28	_____ / 19	_____ / 11

The Periodic Table

Key

relative atomic mass
atomic symbol
name
atomic (proton) number

1	2											3	4	5	6	7	0
						1 **H** hydrogen 1											4 **He** helium 2
7 **Li** lithium 3	9 **Be** beryllium 4											11 **B** boron 5	12 **C** carbon 6	14 **N** nitrogen 7	16 **O** oxygen 8	19 **F** fluorine 9	20 **Ne** neon 10
23 **Na** sodium 11	24 **Mg** magnesium 12											27 **Al** aluminium 13	28 **Si** silicon 14	31 **P** phosphorus 15	32 **S** sulfur 16	35.5 **Cl** chlorine 17	40 **Ar** argon 18
39 **K** potassium 19	40 **Ca** calcium 20	45 **Sc** scandium 21	48 **Ti** titanium 22	51 **V** vanadium 23	52 **Cr** chromium 24	55 **Mn** manganese 25	56 **Fe** iron 26	59 **Co** cobalt 27	59 **Ni** nickel 28	63.5 **Cu** copper 29	65 **Zn** zinc 30	70 **Ga** gallium 31	73 **Ge** germanium 32	75 **As** arsenic 33	79 **Se** selenium 34	80 **Br** bromine 35	84 **Kr** krypton 36
85 **Rb** rubidium 37	88 **Sr** strontium 38	89 **Y** yttrium 39	91 **Zr** zirconium 40	93 **Nb** niobium 41	96 **Mo** molybdenum 42	[98] **Tc** technetium 43	101 **Ru** ruthenium 44	103 **Rh** rhodium 45	106 **Pd** palladium 46	108 **Ag** silver 47	112 **Cd** cadmium 48	115 **In** indium 49	119 **Sn** tin 50	122 **Sb** antimony 51	128 **Te** tellurium 52	127 **I** iodine 53	131 **Xe** xenon 54
133 **Cs** caesium 55	137 **Ba** barium 56	139 **La*** lanthanum 57	178 **Hf** hafnium 72	181 **Ta** tantalum 73	184 **W** tungsten 74	186 **Re** rhenium 75	190 **Os** osmium 76	192 **Ir** iridium 77	195 **Pt** platinum 78	197 **Au** gold 79	201 **Hg** mercury 80	204 **Tl** thallium 81	207 **Pb** lead 82	209 **Bi** bismuth 83	[209] **Po** polonium 84	[210] **At** astatine 85	[222] **Rn** radon 86
[223] **Fr** francium 87	[226] **Ra** radium 88	[227] **Ac*** actinium 89	[261] **Rf** rutherfordium 104	[262] **Db** dubnium 105	[266] **Sg** seaborgium 106	[264] **Bh** bohrium 107	[277] **Hs** hassium 108	[268] **Mt** meitnerium 109	[271] **Ds** darmstadtium 110	[272] **Rg** roentgenium 111							

Elements with atomic numbers 112–116 have been reported but not fully authenticated

*The Lanthanoids (atomic numbers 58–71) and the Actinoids (atomic numbers 90–103) have been omitted.

Cu and **Cl** have not been rounded to the nearest whole number.

Answers

Getting the Energy your Body Needs

Pages 4–15

Vocabulary Builder

1.
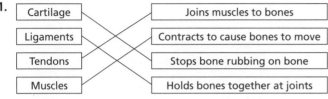

Cartilage		Joins muscles to bones
Ligaments		Contracts to cause bones to move
Tendons		Stops bone rubbing on bone
Muscles		Holds bones together at joints

[3 marks if four or three correct; 2 marks if two correct; 1 mark if one correct]

2. a) False [1]; True [1]
   b) True [1]; True [1]
   c) True [1]; True [1]
   d) False [1]; True [1]

> Plants respire, as well as animals, and so they need mitochondria.

3. a) oxygen [1] b) ethanol [1] c) fracture [1]
   d) blood cells [1] e) lactic acid [1]

Maths Skills

1. a) increases / goes up [1]; more [1]; two [1]
   b) **Accept one from:** males are often heavier; males are less likely to have osteoporosis [1]
   c) i) To have an operation [1]
      ii) Would advise them to reduce risks [1]
      iii) **Any one from:** Older people are more at risk of complications from an operation; older people are likely to have a longer recovery time; the risks of an operation do not outweigh the benefits of the operation. [1]
      iv) The advice would be to have an operation [1]; her risk of having a fracture is 10% [1]

2. a)
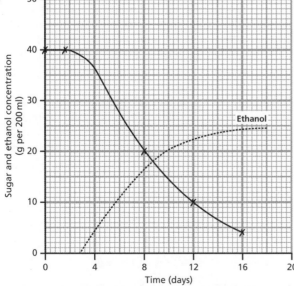

[2 marks for all six points correctly plotted; 1 mark for only five correctly plotted points] [Plus 1 mark for a smooth line drawn]

b) It increases [1]; then starts to level off [1]

> Remember to look at the number of marks for a question – this question has two marks so just 'increases' cannot be the full answer.

c) Approx. 8.8 days [1]

> The answer is at the intersection of the two lines.

d) $4 \times \dfrac{5000}{200}$ [1]
   $= 100\,g$ [1]

Testing Understanding

1.
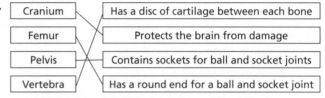

Cranium		Has a disc of cartilage between each bone
Femur		Protects the brain from damage
Pelvis		Contains sockets for ball and socket joints
Vertebra		Has a round end for a ball and socket joint

[3 marks if four or three correct; 2 marks if two correct; 1 mark if one correct]

2. a) 92 seconds [1]
   b) slower [1]; lactic acid [1]; hurt (**Accept** fatigue or cramp) [1]; oxygen (**Accept** O_2) [1]
   c) i) $7.5 \div 5 \times 100$ [1]
         $= 150\%$ [1]
      ii) **Any three from:** they will get more red blood cells; this will allow them to carry more oxygen in the blood; they will be able to have more aerobic respiration; less anaerobic respiration; less lactic acid made [3]

3. a) $14\,000 \div 200$ [1] $= 70$ (times) [1]
   b) Ligaments need to be strong to hold the bones together / prevent dislocation [1]; Tendons need to be strong to allow muscles to pull on bones [1].
   c) Cartilage is not as strong as bone [1]; it would not be able to support the animal. [1]

4. a) glucose/sugar/fructose [1]

> The main sugar in fruit is called fructose.

b) carbon dioxide (**Accept** CO_2) [1]
   c) The microbes might kill/compete with the yeast [1]; they might make other substances that taste nasty/ are poisonous [1].

5. a) i) X = bicep [1]
         Y = tricep [1]
         Z = humerus [1]
      ii) X [1]

> The bicep is called the flexor muscle because it bends or flexes the arm.

b) $(0.033 \times 6 \times 60) + 60$ [1]
   $= 71.88$ [1]
   So, Jo has the strongest bicep [1]

Working Scientifically

1. a) a stopclock/timer [1]
   b) The time since the start of the exercise ✓ [1]

> Remember, the independent variable is the factor that the students choose to vary.

c) $76 \div 4$ **[1]**
   $= 19$ **[1]**
d) Round 2 **[1]**; because it was far too high/ anomalous **[1]**.

> When it is clear that a result does not fit the pattern, it is often left out when calculating the mean.

e) He would plot the mean number of squeezes against time **[1]**; time on the x-axis and squeezes on the y-axis. **[1]**

> Remember, the independent variable is plotted on the x-axis.

f) down **[1]**; 65–75 **[1]**; 75–90 **[1]**; aerobic **[1]**; oxygen **[1]**; lactic acid **[1]**; anaerobic **[1]**

Science in Use
1. a) fermentation/anaerobic respiration **[1]**
   b) glucose → ethanol/alcohol + carbon dioxide **[2]**
   c) **Accept one from:** there's not enough sunshine; it's not warm enough **[1]**
   d) **Any two from:** Petrol is produced very slowly; more ethanol can be made by growing more sugar cane; ethanol can be a renewable biofuel; petrol is non-renewable/finite. **[2]**
   e) 10 litres **[1]**
   f) They will not need to use more land to grow crops **[1]**; therefore, they will not need to cut down more forests. **[1]**
2. a) They will have less cartilage on the ends of their bones **[1]**; so the bones will rub together. **[1]**
   b) The noise is caused by the bones rubbing together **[1]**; the more severe the osteoarthritis then the less cartilage that is present. **[1]**
   c) **Any two from:** It can be done more quickly/less wait; It is sometimes difficult to see how much damage there is on an X-ray; cheaper; no risk of radiation exposure **[2]**

Looking at Plants and Ecosystems

Pages 16–26

Vocabulary Builder
1. root hair cells **[1]**; minerals **[1]**; xylem **[1]**; stomata **[1]**; transpiration **[1]**
2. N = nitrogen **[1]**; P = phosphorus **[1]**; K = potassium **[1]**

> Some elements do not start with the same letter as their symbol because the symbol may refer to their Latin name.

3.
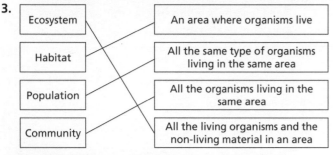

[3 marks if four or three correct; 2 marks if two correct; 1 mark if one correct]

4. a) True **[1]**; True **[1]**; False **[1]**
   b) False **[1]**; False **[1]**; True **[1]**
   c) False **[1]**; True **[1]**; True **[1]**

Maths Skills
1. a) i)   4000 **[1]**
      ii) 3000 **[1]**
   b) 8000 + 4000 **[1]**
      = 12 000 **[1]**
   c) Organic **[1]**; intensive farming only needs 11 250 megajoules **[1]**
2. a) 40 **[1]**

> The mean is 39, so in order to get this mean, the three readings must be 40, 39 and 38.

   b) The number of bubbles was much lower/anomalous result. **[1]**
   c)
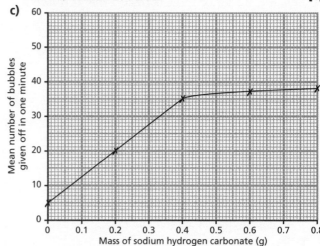

[2 marks for all five points correctly plotted; 1 mark for only four points correctly plotted] [Plus 1 mark for a smooth line drawn]

   d) increases **[1]**; carbon dioxide **[1]**; photosynthesis **[1]**; level off **[1]**

Testing Understanding
1. a) ladybird **[1]**
   b) i)   The greenfly will not eat the wheat **[1]**; so the farmer will get a larger yield **[1]**
      ii) **Any three from:** more mice as they have more wheat to eat; fewer ladybirds as fewer greenfly to eat; fewer blue tits as fewer ladybirds to eat; blue tits might die due to bioaccumulation of the pesticide **[3]**
2. a) A = upper epidermis **[1]**; B = palisade mesophyll **[1]**; C = spongy mesophyll **[1]**; D = lower epidermis **[1]**
   b) B **[1]**
   c) **Any two from:** evergreen: thicker waxy cuticles; fewer stomata; two layers of palisade cells; is thicker **[2]**
3. a) rice plants ⟶ humans

      azolla ⟶ fish

   [1 mark for organisms correctly connected; 1 mark for correct direction of arrows]

> Remember that the direction of the arrows shows the movement of food or energy through the food web.

   b) It acts as a fertiliser / provides minerals **[1]**; for the plants to produce amino acids/proteins. **[1]**

c) The insects feed off the rice plants [1]; so removing them will increase the rice yield. [1]

> A parasite feeds on or in a living organism, causing it harm.

4. a) The leaves cannot photosynthesise and make any starch [1]; the starch present is used by the plant. [1]

> Keeping a plant in the dark is called destarching.

b) i) iodine solution ✓ [1]

ii) B [1]

iii) The black areas indicate starch [1]; only black where light hits the leaf [1]; only black where there is chlorophyll [1].

Working Scientifically

1. a) i) **Any two from:** shoots came from the same plant; shoots have the same number of leaves; they left the shoots for the same time [2]

> Remember, a fair test means that every factor is kept constant apart from the factors being tested. This makes the results **valid**.

ii) To stop water evaporating from the test tube. ✓ [1]

iii) As a control / to see if water was being lost from the leaves. [1]

b) i) 1.6 [1]; 0.2 [1]

ii) A [1]

iii) All the leaves are in place [1]; no grease is on the leaves [1].

iv) Stomata are mainly on the lower surface [1]; the stomata are blocked by the grease [1].

2. a) 52 ÷ 4 [1]
= 13 [1]

b) The increase in fertiliser added causes an increase in reproduction [1]; there is a large increase up to 2 g but less increase at greater amounts [1].

c) **Accept any two from:** to make it a fair test; increased light might increase rate of reproduction; as the duckweed would have more food [2]

> The question asks you to 'explain', so just writing 'to make it a fair test' will not get full marks.

Science in Use

1. a) The numbers of the organism are very low [1]; the organism may become extinct [1].

b) **Any two from:** outcompetes the white-clawed crayfish; eats its food; eats the white-clawed crayfish [2]

c) 5000 × 10 ÷ 100 [1]
= 500 [1]

d) To stop people visiting it [1]; otherwise they might disturb the crayfish / catch them / accidently introduce the North American crayfish [1].

e) **Any two from:** best (optimum) habitat will have been created; plenty of food present; no predators; no North American crayfish present; less pollution [2]

Explaining Physical Changes

Pages 27–38

Vocabulary Builder

1. a)

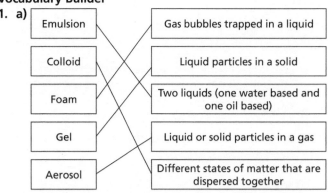

[4 marks if five or four correct; 3 marks if three correct; 2 marks if two correct; 1 mark if one correct]

2. hypothesis [1]; peer review [1]; repeat [1]; hypothesis [1]; scientific theory [1]

3. a) i) A [1]

ii) B [1]

iii) D [1]

iv) B [1]

v) C [1]

b)

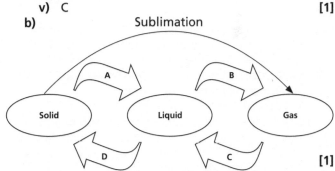

[1]

4. A: The measure of the number of solute particles in a given volume of solvent. [1]

5. a) T [1]

b) F [1]

c) T [1]

Maths Skills

1. a) density = mass ÷ volume [1]

b) density = 14 ÷ 10 [1]
= 1.4 [1] g/cm³ [1]

c) mass = density × volume [1]
= 10 × 1 [1]
= 10 [1] g [1]

> Density is a measure of how many particles there are in a given space.

d) volume = mass ÷ density [1]
= 55 ÷ 1 [1] = 55 [1] cm³ [1]

e) Cooking oil will float on water [1]; because cooking oil is less dense than water / cooking oil has a lower density than water / water is denser than cooking oil / water has a higher density than oil [1].

2. a) minutes [1]

b) 55°C [1]

c) 90°C [1]

d) solid [1]
e) liquid [1]
3. **a)** Borosilicate, sodalime, glass window [1]
   b) 6 [1]
   c) 8 [1]
   d) (6 + 5.5 + 7.5) ÷ 3 [1]
       = 6.33333333 [1]
       = 6.33 [1]

> Make sure you read the question carefully and present the answer to the correct decimal places.

4. **a)** Solubility [1]
   b) °C [1]
   c) As temperature increases, the solubility of oxygen decreases. [1]
5. **a)** Liquid [1]
   b) Solid [1]
   c) Gas [1]

Testing Understanding

1. **a)** The carbon particle moves randomly [1] in all directions/in random directions [1].
   b) Brownian motion [1]
   c) The liquid particles move and collide with (each other and) the sides of the container [1]. Pressure is a measure of the average force [1] of these collisions over the area of the container's sides [1].
2. **a)** diffusion [1]
   b) The perfume particles are in high concentration near the perfume bottle [1]. Particles move from an area of high concentration to an area of low concentration/with the concentration gradient [1]; until there is no overall change in concentration/equilibrium happens [1].
   c) The temperature will be higher on a summer's day compared to a winter's day [1]; so the particles will move faster [1]; diffusion happens faster [1]; and the smell spreads out faster [1].
3. **a)** Physical change [1]. No new substance is made [1].
   b) It is endothermic. [1]
   c) 101g [1]
   d) evaporate the water/crystalise [1]
4. **a)** Chemical [1]. A new substance is made [1] as there is a colour change [1].
   b) 1.2g – 0.8g [1]
       = 0.4g [1]
   c) copper(II) carbonate [1] → copper(II) oxide + carbon dioxide [1]
5. **a)** T [1]
   b) F [1]
   c) T [1]
   d) T [1]
   e) F [1]
   f) F [1]
   g) T [1]
6. **a)** The heating transfers the energy to the particles in the copper [1]. This causes them to increase their vibrations / increase frequency and amplitude of the vibration [1]. As the particles vibrate more, each takes up more space [1].

b)

[1 mark for showing particles in a random arrangement; 1 mark for showing most of the particles touching]

Working Scientifically

1. **a)** top pan balance (**Do not accept** scale) [1]
   b)

Material	Mass (g)
Iron	
Brick	
Lead	

[1 mark for 'Material' heading in the first column; 1 mark for first column completed; 1 mark for 'Mass' heading in the second column; 1 mark for (g) given as the unit in the second column]

   c)

Material	Mass (g)
Iron	7.9
Brick	1.4
Lead	11.3

[1 mark for the three correct numbers only – do not give mark if the unit is written with the quantity]
   d) 1 [1] cm^3 [1]
2. **a)** measuring cylinder [1]
   b) 1 ml = 1 cm^3 [1] so 10 ml = 10 cm^3 [1]
   c) 13 ÷ 10 [1] = 1.3 [1] g/cm^3 [1]
3. **a)** thermometer [1]
   b) time [1]
   c) temperature [1]
   d) The candle wax could burn the skin if it touched it [1].
   e) The candle wax was heated past the boiling point [1]. This caused it to turn into a gas [1] and be lost to the atmosphere [1].
4. **a)** Goggles/eye protection [1] and gloves [1] because sodium hydroxide is corrosive [1].
   b) a beaker (**Accept** conical flask) [1]
   c) 5 ÷ 100 [1]
       = 0.05 [1] g/cm^3 [1]

Science in Use

1. **a)** 0.5% [1]
   b) steel [1], bronze [1]
   c) Steel is magnetic/iron is magnetic and found in steel [1]. Bronze is not magnetic because copper, tin and zinc are not magnetic [1]. Only modern 1p and 2p coins have steel/magnetic metal in them [1].

d)

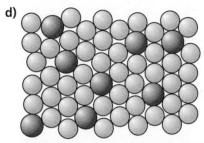

[1 mark for particles closely packed; 1 mark for two different sizes of particles randomly arranged]

   e) The different sizes of atoms make it more difficult for the layers of atoms to slide over each other. [1]
2. **a)** A: condensation [1]
      B: evaporation [1]
   b) A physical change [1]; because no new substance is made [1].
   c) Denser materials sink in less dense liquids/gases/fluids [1]. Ice is less dense than liquid water [1].

Explaining Chemical Changes

Pages 39–48

Vocabulary Builder
1. **a)**

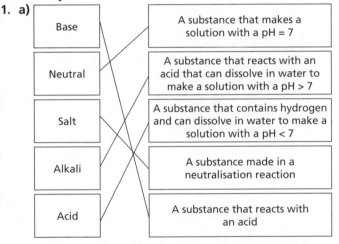

[4 marks if five or four correct; 3 marks if three correct; 2 marks if two correct; 1 mark if one correct]
2. burning [1]; energy [1]; Hydrocarbons [1]; petrol [1]; natural gas [1]
3. A chemical that is a different colour [1] in an acid or alkali solution [1].
4. **a)** complete combustion (**Accept** oxidation) [1]
   b) neutralisation [1]
   c) oxidation [1]
   d) neutralisation [1]
   e) incomplete combustion (**Accept** oxidation) [1]
5. Antacid ✓ [1]
6. **a)** F [1]
   b) T [1]
   c) F [1]
   d) F [1]
   e) T [1]

Maths Skills
1. **a)** 163.8 g [1]
   b) 163.8 − 161.4 [1]
      = 2.4 g [1]
   c) 1 minute = 60 seconds [1]
      60 × 20 = 1200 seconds [1]

   d) 1 kg = 1000 g [1]
      0.01 × 1000 = 10 g [1]
2. **a)** × 10 [1]
   b) × 100 [1]
   c) × 1000 [1]
   d) × 10 000 [1]
3. **a)** 28 000 000 [1]
   b) Manufacture of fertilisers [1]
   c) 0.1 × 28 000 000 [1]
      = 2 800 000 [1]
      = 2.8 × 10⁶ [1]

   Make sure you read a question carefully so you don't lose marks for not presenting the answer to the correct decimal place or standard form.

   d) 5% [1]

Testing Understanding
1. **a)** Sulfuric acid [1]
   b) Nitric acid [1]
   c) chloride [1]
   d) nitrate [1]
2. **a)** oxygen [1]
   b) water [1]
   c) magnesium [1]
   d) hydrochloric acid [1]
   e) **Accept in either order:** potassium sulfate [1]; water [1]
3. **a)** **Accept in either order:** A: oxygen [1]; B: heat [1]
   b) methane + oxygen → carbon dioxide + water **[1 mark for correct reactants; 1 mark for correct products]**

   Remember that word equations should be written so that the reactants or starting chemicals are always on the left of the arrow and the products are always on the right.

   c) methane + oxygen → water + carbon/soot + carbon monoxide
      (Also accept carbon dioxide for a product) **[1 mark for correct reactants; 1 mark for correct products]**
   d)

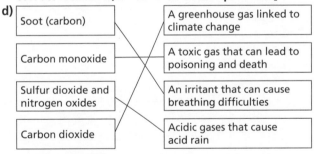

   [3 marks if four or three correct; 2 marks if two correct; 1 mark if one correct]
4. **a) i)** **Accept in either order:** hydrogen [1]; salt [1]
      ii) **Accept in any order:** carbon dioxide [1]; water [1]; salt [1]
      iii) **Accept in either order:** salt [1]; water [1]
      iv) **Accept in either order:** salt [1]; water [1]
   b) i) Use a lit splint [1]. You will hear a pop [1].
      ii) Use limewater [1], which turns from colourless [1] to cloudy [1].
5. **a)** sodium carbonate + hydrochloric acid → sodium chloride + carbon dioxide + water **[1 mark for correct reactants; 1 mark for correct products]**

b) i) pink/red/orange/yellow [1]
    ii) blue/purple [1]
    iii) green [1]
c) A gas/carbon dioxide gas was made. [1]
d) neutralisation [1]

Working Scientifically

1. a) measuring cylinder [1]
  b) conical flask [1]
  c) To stop spray from escaping [1]
  d) mass [1]
  e) Mass will decrease [1] as a gas (carbon dioxide) is made and lost to the atmosphere [1]. When the reaction is complete [1] the mass will not change further [1].
2. a) Take a sample of the substance [1]. Add a few drops of universal indicator solution/put the tip of universal indicator paper into the sample [1]. Note the colour of the indicator [1] and compare with the colour chart to find the pH value [1].
  b)

Substance	Colour	pH
lemon juice	red	2
cola	orange	3
tomato juice	orange	4
water	green	7
baking soda	dark green	9

[1 mark for adding the three column labels: Substance (the independent variable), Colour, pH; 1 mark for all data correctly written in the table]
3. a) the difference in pH/colour change [1]; the time it takes for the reaction to complete [1]
  b) use the same type/concentration/volume of acid [1]; use the recommended dosage for each antacid [1]; keep the temperature the same [1].
  c) wear eye protection [1]; wash hands after completing experiment [1]
  d) Litmus can only tell you if a solution is an acid or an alkali [1]. It doesn't show the change in pH/difference in acidity levels [1].

Science in Use

1. a) base [1]
  b) neutralisation [1]
  c) universal indicator [1]

Remember that only universal indicator can be used to determine the pH. All other indicators just tell you if something is an acid or an alkali but not its pH.

  d) pH probe [1]

Indicators are chemicals which are called reagents as they are needed for the chemical analysis. But scientific equipment refers to instruments or glassware needed for the experiment. So, indicators are reagents and not equipment.

  e) calcium oxide + water → calcium hydroxide
  [1 mark for correct reactants, 1 mark for correct products]
  f) an alkali (**Accept** base) [1]
2. a) It contains only [1] carbon and hydrogen [1].
  b) oxygen [1]

c) Black powder is soot/carbon [1], which shows that incomplete combustion has been happening [1]. This can also make carbon monoxide [1], which is a toxic gas [1].

Exploring Contact and Non-contact Forces

Pages 49–58

Vocabulary Builder

1. a) Accept any three from: friction; aerodynamic lift; tension; air resistance; drag [3]
  b) Accept any three from: magnetic; gravity; weight; electric [3]
2. a) repulsive [1] **b)** attractive [1] **c)** repulsive [1]
3. a) gravitational [1] **b)** electric [1]
  c) gravitational [1] **d)** magnetic [1]
4. electron ✓ [1]
5. iron ✓ [1]
6. a) bottom ✓ [1]
  b) Liquid pressure is greater at a greater depth. [1]
7. a) up ✓ [1] **b)** upthrust ✓ [1]
8. a) false [1] **b)** true [1] **c)** true [1]

Maths Skills

1. weight = (3 × 10) = 30 N [1]

The Earth's gravitational field strength is 10 N/kg. This means that the Earth exerts a force of gravity of 10 newtons on a 1 kilogram mass.

2. a) force = (5 × 10) = 50 N [1]
  b) force = (2 × 10) = 20 N [1]
3. a) area = (0.60 × 0.50) = 0.30 m^2 [1]

The area of a rectangular surface is equal to its length multiplied by its width.

  b) pressure = (30 ÷ 0.30) = 100 N/m^2 [1]

The formula of 'pressure = force ÷ area' can also be written: $p = \dfrac{F}{A}$

4. a) force = (70 × 10) = 700 N [1]
  b) pressure = (700 ÷ 0.07) = 10 000 N/m^2 [1]
  c) pressure = 20 000 N/m^2 [1]
5. force = (2 × 100 000) = 200 000 N [1]
6. a)–b)

a) [1 mark for point correctly plotted]
b) [1 mark for single smooth curved line drawn through the points]
c) between 8.5 and 8.8 ✓ [1]
d) A gravitational field created by either the Sun, or a planet, or a moon. [1]

Testing Understanding

1. a) Vertical arrow from centre of container, pointing downwards [1]
   b) 25 N ✓ [1]
   c) i) true [1]
      ii) false [1]
      iii) true [1]
2. force = (30 × 10) = 300 N [1]; direction = upwards [1]
3. a) true [1]
   b) false [1]
   c) false [1]
   d) true [1]
4. a) repulsive [1]
   b) repulsive [1]
   c) attractive [1]

   Opposite poles attract, and opposite charges attract.

5. Charge on rod A is positive. [1]; The force between the rods is repulsive [1] so the rods must have the same type of charge [1].
6. a) electrons [1]
   b) electric [1]
   c) Accept either: The cloth loses electrons; The cloth becomes positively charged. [1]
7. a) true [1]
   b) false [1]
   c) true [1]
8. a) Jets C and D [1]; Jet D comes from the hole at the greater depth and travels furthest horizontally/to the right [1].
   b) Jets A and B [1]; The holes are at the same depth and the jets travel the same distance [1].
9. a) The force arrows are longer at a greater depth. [1]
   b) upthrust; weight [1]

Working Scientifically

1. a) Without the adjustment, the newton-meter would give incorrect measurements. [1]

   Alternative names for a newton-meter include spring-balance and force-meter.

   b) 1.0 [1]
   c) 0.6 [1]
   d) Liquid pressure increases with depth [1]. The force exerted by the liquid on the bottom surface of the pebble is greater than on the top surface [1].
   e) A: a eureka can (Accept displacement can) [1]
      B: a measuring cylinder [1]
   f) weight = (61 × 0.0098) = 0.6 N (Accept 0.5978 N) [1]

Science in Use

1. a) Accept either answer: Because the weight of the greatest depth of atmosphere acts at sea level; Because the density of the air is greater at sea level. [1]
   b) Accept value in the range: 50 < value < 57 kN/m² [1]
   c) air resistance (Accept drag or friction.) [1]

d) So they know when to open their parachute. [1]
e) Accept either answer: The atmosphere at this altitude does not contain enough oxygen molecules; The air is thinner at this altitude. [1]
f) Accept any number less than 32 (Do not accept 'zero') [1]

Magnetism and Electricity

Pages 59–71

Vocabulary Builder

1. a) Accept one from: Iron, Copper, Aluminium, Steel [1]
   b) Accept one from: Polythene, PVC, Polystyrene [1]
   c) Accept one from: Polythene, PVC [1]
   d) Steel [1]
   e) Iron [1]
2. a) If the nail is magnetised it will attract iron filings. [1]
   b) If the nail is magnetised, the compass needle will point towards one end of the nail but away from the other end. [1]
3. a) B: switch [1]; C: lamp [1]; D: lead [1]
   b) i) chemical [1]; light [1]
      ii) resistance [1]
      iii) potential difference [1]
4. a) Ammeter [1]
   b)

   [1 mark for each of the four components correctly drawn up to a maximum of 4 marks]
   c) voltmeter [1]
   d) ohm ✓ [1]

Maths Skills

1. a) Accept potential difference in the range: 5.6 to 5.8 [1]; volt or V [1]
   b) Accept electric current in the range: 1.2 to 1.4 [1]; amp or A [1]
   c) Accept resistance correctly calculated from answers to a) and b) [1] (Note, the value will be in the range from 4.0 to 4.9 ohm)

   The formula of 'resistance = potential difference ÷ electric current' can also be written as $R = \dfrac{V}{I}$.

2. a) Z ✓ [1]
   b) X ✓ [1]
3. a) (60 × 60) = 3600 s [1]
   b) energy = (10 × 3600) = 36 000 J [1]
   c) less than 1 pence ✓ [1]
4. a) electrical; thermal [2]
   b) energy = (2000 × 60 × 60) = 7 200 000 J [1]
5. a) i) 2300 [1]
      ii) 1.15 [1]
      iii) 57.5 [1]
      iv) 230 [1]
   b) kettle [1]

   Reminder: the highest power appliance costs the most to run per second.

Testing Understanding

1. a) bar magnet [1]
   b) compass [1]
   c) **Accept one suitable example, e.g.:** navigation; map reading [1]
2. a) Y ✓ [1]
   b) W ✓ [1]
   c) Y ✓ [1]
   d) X ✓ [1]
   e) Z ✓ [1]
3. a) The electric current in the wire magnetises the nail [1]. The compass needles align themselves with the nail's magnetic field [1].
   b) The point of the nail is a south pole [1]. A compass needle points into a south pole [1].
   c) All would again point in a northerly direction. [1]
4. 0.06 A ✓ [1]

> In a circuit, the current leaving a battery is equal in size to the current returning to the battery.

5. 0.05 A ✓ [1]

> In a circuit, the current entering a junction is equal to the current leaving the junction.

6. 0.05 A ✓ [1]
7. S_1 and S_3 [1]
8.

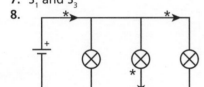

[1 mark for each correct additional arrow up to maximum of 3 marks]

> When labelling the current direction in a circuit, remember to show the current leaving the positive terminal of the battery/cell and returning to the negative terminal.

9. a) resistance = (2 ÷ 0.10) = 20 ohms [1]
   b) 0.20 A ✓ [1]
10. a) resistance = (1.2 ÷ 0.020) = 60 ohms [1]
    b)

[1]

11. a) 0.030 A ✓ [1]
    b) 0.0075 A ✓ [1]
    c) Circuit Y [1]; circuit Y draws a smaller current from the cell than circuit X [1].

Working Scientifically

1. a) electromagnet [1]
   b) It disappears. [1]
   c) i) mass = (20 + 250) = 270 g [1]
      ii) total mass = (270 g + 30 g = 300 g) = 0.30 kg
          (**Accept** 0.3 kg) [1]
      iii) weight = (0.30 × 10) = 3.0 N [1]

d)

Total mass (kilograms)	Total weight needed to pull the plate off the core (newtons)
0.30	3.0
0.24	2.4
0.18	1.8
0.12	1.2
0.06	0.6

[1 mark for each correct row, up to a maximum of 5 marks]

e)–f)

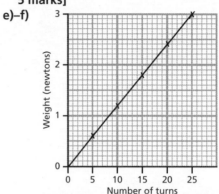

[1 mark for each correctly plotted point, up to maximum of 5 marks] [1 mark for a correctly drawn straight line]

g) Accept answer in the range: 2.1 to 2.2 N [1]

h)

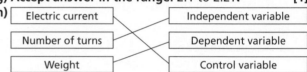

[2 marks if three correct, 1 mark if two or one correct]

Science in Use

1. a) i) 5 [1]
      ii) 20 [1]
   b) i) **Accept any two suitable examples, e.g.:** tumble dryer; microwave; food mixer; fan [2]
      ii) **Accept two suitable examples, e.g.:** tram; milk float; electric train; electric scooter [2]
   c) i) coil [1]
      ii) electric [1]; magnetic [1]
      iii) clockwise [1]
   d) **Accept one suitable advantage, e.g.:** Does not emit exhaust gases; Improves air quality in towns and cities; Reduces noise pollution in towns and cities; Helps reduce levels of greenhouse gases in the atmosphere. [1]